C000214138

The
Hereford &
Gloucester
Canal

by
David Bick

with a contribution on the
GLOUCESTER TO LEDBURY RAILWAY
by John Norris

THE OAKWOOD PRESS

First published 1979
Second Edition 1994
New Edition 2003
© Oakwood Press & David Bick 2003

British Library Cataloguing in Publication Data
A Record for this book is available from the British Library
ISBN 0 85361 599 3

Typeset by Oakwood Graphics.
Repro by Ford Graphics, Ringwood, Hants.
Printed by Stourprint Ltd, Blandford, Dorset.

In Memory of Stephen Ballard, Engineer.

This charming watercolour is the work of Philip Ballard and dated 30th January, 1838. It is probably the earliest example of a barge-cabin with painted decorations.

Title page: Deep waters. Looking north inside Oxenhall tunnel *c.*1970. *Author's Collection*

Front cover, top: Lock Cottage, Oxenhall, and the lock undergoing restoration.
Author's Collection
Front cover, bottom: John Kemp's painting showing the canal at Over, with Gloucester cathedral in the distance. *Gloucester Museum & Art Gallery*
Rear cover, top: The restored canal above Lock Cottage, Oxenhall. *Author*
Rear cover, bottom: A fine stretch of canal two miles north of Ledbury. *Author*

Published by The Oakwood Press (Usk), P.O. Box 13, Usk, Mon., NP15 1YS.
E-mail: oakwood-press@dial.pipex.com
Website: www.oakwood-press.dial.pipex.com

Contents

The Ellbrook aqueduct near Lock Cottage, Oxenhall, about 1980.   *Author*

Gloucester Docks c.1910. The warehouses on the left are now demolished. The far warehouse is now the offices of Gloucester City Council. *Author's Collection*

Foreword to Second Edition

To meet old friends is always pleasurable; so it is with David Bick and the Hereford & Gloucester Canal. Over 40 years ago I noted the canal's line across Alney Island; then with my canal-accustomed wife I cycled from Ludlow to find Walsopthorne tunnel - easily done once we had spotted the spoil heaps.

I did not know whether the canal had ever reached Hereford until we ordered tea from a menu surrounded by advertisements. One named a firm at 'The Wharf'. I could hardly finish my tea before dragging her off to find the old basins. There they were much as they had been left long before.

Later David Bick showed us much more: I remember both ends of Oxenhall tunnel, and tracing the line of the branch round the church.

It is all recalled, and much more given, by this new edition of his book, including his account of the work of the Hereford and Gloucester Canal Trust. To see parts of the old canal brought back to life with boats on them is a pleasure to a veteran such as I, for moving boats have always been my yardstick in judging restoration work. Good fortune to David Bick's enlarged book and to seeing more moving boats over longer lengths of canal.

Charles Hadfield (1994)

Restoration at Oxenhall. This is the only complete lock remaining on the canal.   *Brian Fox*

Introduction to First and Third Editions

'I will not call the canal a liberal education; it was more of an invitation to enquiry, an enquiry that could not then be followed, whatever wonders it offered. It was Romance to me'.
John Masefield

Throughout the length and breadth of England, no major navigation is so lost in obscurity as the Hereford & Gloucester Canal. Unlike its famous neighbour, the Thames & Severn, with which comparisons may be drawn, all links with living memory have inevitably broken and apart from a brief account here and there, its story has never been told. Small wonder then, that these 34 miles of inland waterway are a thing forgotten.

Promoted on a doubtful footing during the Canal Mania of the 1790s, the Hereford & Gloucester Canal has an absorbing history and industrial archaeology, and it is hoped these pages will provide a useful introduction to a subject which I have studied on and off for 30 years.

In particular, reference is made at some length to the part played by Stephen Ballard, a local man by whose drive and ability the canal was at last completed, and whose diaries have provided a vivid insight into days before the railways came. For one who numbered among his friends and acquaintances George and Robert Stephenson, Thomas Brassey, Joseph Locke, and I.K. Brunel, Ballard's name, like the canal he built, has lapsed into undeserved oblivion. The biographical notes included here are an attempt to restore his position among the foremost contractors and engineers of the day.

No story of the canal would be complete without reference to the Gloucester-Ledbury railway, which after 1885 assumed to a considerable extent its role and route, and a chapter on this era has been kindly contributed by John Norris.

Of the canal itself, many remnants survive to surprise those who care to leave the beaten track - bridges, aqueducts, tunnels, and silent ribbons of water which we can scarcely believe no barge has parted for a hundred years. Yet in this age of restoration wonders, who can be sure those waters will not part again?

Finally, an explanation. Although the official title was the Herefordshire & Gloucestershire Canal Navigation Company, the canal itself was often known simply as the Hereford & Gloucester, and this distinction will generally be observed throughout.

Introduction to the Third Edition

I am grateful to my publishers for allowing a revision and the chance to include many new illustrations. Not least is material recording the achievements of the Herefordshire & Gloucestershire Canal Trust in its endeavours to link two cities by water again, after a gap of well over a century.

Chapter One

Before the Canal

Rivers had from time immemorial been an important highway for trade, especially for minerals and heavy goods, although they were often ill-suited to the purpose. Their shortcomings included natural obstructions such as shallows and rapids, as well as trees on the banks which interfered with towing. Man-made weirs associated with mills also caused trouble, demanding trans-shipment of the cargo unless the vessel was small enough to manhandle or winch across. However, such obstructions created a good stretch of water above them, an advantage that was not always appreciated until too late.

In addition, a swift-flowing river made haulage of 'uphill' traffic an arduous business, and its often sinuous route drew out the journey greatly. As to this, no better example might be found than the Wye, that most beautiful of rivers, which takes 70 miles from Hereford to the Severn, though a crow might fly it in twenty-nine.

Many were the attempts at improvement. Dams and weirs proved a continual irritant and in 1661 an Act relating to both the Wye and Lugg was passed enabling pound-locks to be provided at each - the best solution. But only one was built on the Wye, at New Weir near Symond's Yat, and only this remained when by a further Act, obstructions were removed in another attempt to aid traffic.

But in 1727 an Act of George I authorised new mills and weirs, now to improve navigation, and thus turning the wheel full circle. Traffic continued as best it could, and boats gradually increased from small flat-bottomed craft holding a few tons in the 1650s to sailing barges of 28 or 30 tons by 1800.

Downward trade was substantial. In 1777 it included 9,000 tons of corn and meal, and 2,000 tons of cider; the main back-carriage was coal from the Forest of Dean below Ross. According to a survey by Robert Whitworth in 1790, there were no less than 11 dams or weirs between Hereford and Monmouth, the distances from the city being quoted as follows:

		miles			miles
1	Below Eign Wharf	1 ½	7	Upper end of Homford	30
2	Below Hampton	4 ½	8	Courtfield Ferry	36
3	By Old Mill	9	9	Near Hadnocks Stream	46
4	Carey Shoal	14	10	Old Weir, Coldwell	-
5	Hoarwithy Ferry	16	11	New Weir, Symond's Yat	-
6	Old Weir	23			

However, though the Wye suited trade with Bristol and the South-West, the distance via Chepstow and the Severn to Gloucester and the Midlands was far greater than by road, and a more direct waterway had long been in contemplation. The main obstacle was the Malvern Hills which lay directly in its path, the only practicable route being via Ledbury, where the inhabitants had attempted to promote a canal to the Severn in 1774.

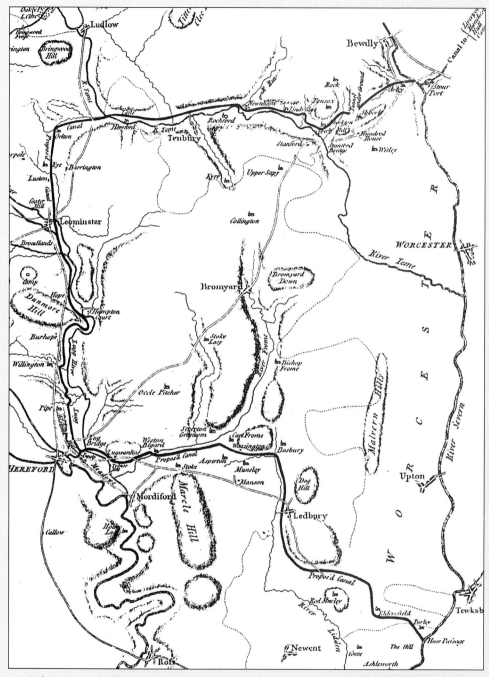

A dream never fulfilled. An ambitious plan for a canal linking Stourport, Leominster, Hereford and Ledbury, re-joining the Severn below Tewkesbury. *Hereford City Library*

Three years later, a pupil of Brindley, Robert Whitworth, suggested a route from Stourport-on-Severn to Leominster and Hereford, thence to the Severn near Gloucester, which formed a semi-circle of 70 miles or more. Only a land-locked part, the Leominster Canal, was eventually built. Then, in 1789, Richard Hall proposed a canal from Hereford via Ledbury and Eldersfield to the Severn above Wainlodes. Shortly afterwards, the course was revised down the Leadon valley to Gloucester, with a branch to Newent. The plan met with general approval, and as we shall see in the next chapter, formed the basis of the canal finally built. Strangely, however, a link with the River Wye which might seem a very obvious and desirable feature, was never included in spite of various arguments advanced in favour.

Once the projected canal became a certainty, hopes of properly converting the Wye were doomed; but since the new development could never entirely replace trade on the river with all those villages and towns so readily served, navigation continued for generations. And the traffic was not only commercial. In 1806, you could hire a pleasure boat at Fownhope worked by three men, and journey to Ross, Monmouth or Chepstow. The cost for the latter trip was no less than four guineas, a very considerable sum in those days. One wonders how long it took.

The lack of a towpath had ever been a handicap, and in 1809 an Act was passed to make one between Hereford and Lydbrook, where much of the Forest coal was shipped. Tolls were not to exceed 6d. per mile for every horse. It was opened in 1811, prior to which boats, sometimes aided by a favourable wind, were bow-hauled by men. A more exhausting or degrading task could scarcely be imagined. Boats sometimes ventured as far upstream as Hay, whilst at Monnington, barges were pulled through the rapids by a windlass.

Every riverside village had its quay, and those at Hereford were thronged with barges. One of the city's industries was ship-building, a brig of 170 tons being launched opposite Castle Green in 1823 and a 64 ton steamer the *Paul Pry*, in 1829. Near Fownhope, barges unloaded coal for local limekilns which were once a substantial business, and similar evidence could be found in many other places.

The final blow came in 1855 when the Hereford, Ross & Gloucester Railway opened. After this, commercial traffic is said to have ceased altogether, though this can hardly be true, since in the 1880s Highmeadow Colliery built a tramway for loading coal onto railway wagons and boats below Symond's Yat. Paradoxically, probably the biggest vessel ever to be seen in Hereford, the 230 ton *Wye Invader*, did not arrive there until 1989. Its passage up the river caused a sensation, and many were the voices that roundly declared the journey impossible, not least due to very tight clearances under bridges, and the rapids at New Weir. The boat, a Dutch barge, was intended for a floating restaurant, and at the time of writing its fate remains in the balance.

As for the River Lugg navigation, it can be dismissed in a few lines, being scarcely worthy of such a title. It is often forgotten that the shrubs and trees which border nearly every river are a great obstacle to a towpath, and need removal, a problem which does not arise with a waterway made for the purpose; how this was overcome with the Lugg is not recorded. In 1714 a Mr

Chinn received £900 to carry out work, but did little effective beyond building a wharf and basin at Eton Bridge, Leominster. Between 1746 and 1748, Leominster Corporation made some improvements and in 1756 church bells from the Priory went to Chepstow and returned by water after re-casting; but the effort proved so fraught that the upper reaches of the river were soon abandoned. A little traffic continued to use the few miles to Lugg Bridge Mills and the wharf there, until about 1850. Traces of locks, or their poor relation, half-locks, can still be seen in a number of places.

It may well be asked, how was it that such a waterway came to exert so strong and enduring a spell over the proprietors of the Hereford & Gloucester Canal? Serving a purely agricultural district with little industry and not a single large town, its chances of contributing to dividends were slender, even if a proper navigation might have been had for nothing. That such a straw was grasped, signified both the optimism of the day and the doubtful basis of the whole concern.

More on the Lugg proposals is given in Chapter Four.

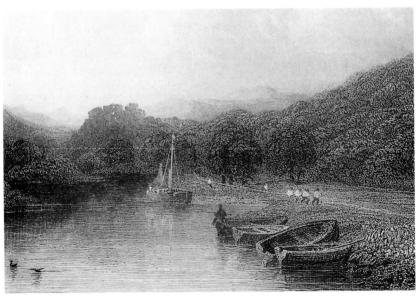

Bow-hauling on the River Wye, with Goodrich Castle in the background, from an original drawing by Peter de Wint.

Chapter Two

Building to Ledbury

Richard Hall's proposal for a canal from Hereford via Ledbury to Gloucester formed the subject of a meeting on 18th March, 1790, when it was agreed to open a subscription for £100 shares. Josiah Clowes was appointed Engineer; he had worked under Whitworth on the newly opened Thames & Severn Canal, and a few weeks later submitted a report confirming Hall's route.

The estimated cost came to a fraction under £70,000 for a canal suitable for boats 70 ft long and 8 ft wide to carry 35 tons cargo with a draught of 3 ft 6 in. The estimate proved of course, much too low, as they always do, for if the truth were told, how many projects on such a scale would ever leave the ground?

The engineering features included a short tunnel near Hereford and a long one at Ashperton, the overall length being 35½ miles. From Ledbury, the route took an easy course down the Leadon Valley to the Severn, which it was intended to cross by an aqueduct, and thence a further ½ mile over Alney Island to Gloucester.

There was also to be a three mile branch to Newent, not so much for its trade, as to exploit nearby deposits of coal which had been worked on a desultory scale since Roman times. Much was made of the potential. In his report, Clowes estimated that no less than 12,000 tons would be annually sent to Hereford, plus 4,000 tons each to Ledbury and Gloucester, or 20,000 tons in all. This amounted to almost half the canal's total estimated revenue; for a tiny coalfield currently raising but a few tons a week in fits and starts, it was optimism indeed.

Fortunately for the promoters a mania for canals was ready to sweep the country, without which it is doubtful if even the prospect of substantial mineral traffic for this dead-end route would have sufficed to lift the venture off the ground. According to a contemporary publication,

It is generally acknowledged that the City of Hereford, and its environs, are great sufferers from the want of a regular supply of Coal. That there are considerable quantities of this commodity, of a superior quality, in the neighbourhood of Newent, is an unquestionable matter of fact. The testimony of colliers, who have worked in the pits for six years without intermission, and that given upon oath, joined to the unanimous consent of the inhabitants of that place, afford a weight of evidence sufficient to satisfy the doubts of the most sceptical inquirer. It is true these pits have not been worked for the last 24 years. This neglect must be attributed to the want of a proper market. But should our present proposal be adopted, the Proprietors will engage to produce, at an easy rate, quantities of Coal, fully adequate to the consumption of this City, and the adjacent country.

As if to convince doubters, a few months later the public was informed that 'additional veins of coal have been discovered so as to leave no apprehension of a scarcity.' It was then unanimously decided to petition Parliament for a Bill, and in April 1791 an Act was passed without amendment for construction by the Herefordshire & Gloucestershire Navigation Company with £75,000 authorised capital and powers to raise £30,000 more. The Act gave a list of 110

To the Gentlemen Promoters of a Navigable CANAL *from the City of* Hereford, *by Way of the Towns of* Ledbury *and* Newent, *to the City of* Glocefter.

GENTLEMEN,

IN purfuance of your directions, I have furveyed the principal part of the Line taken by Mr. HALL, and particularly the difficult parts thereof; and I have alfo furveyed the general Face of the Country between the Cities of Hereford and Glocefter; and I find that the Line taken by Mr. HALL in his laft furvey, agreeable to which the plan is now laid down, is the moft eligible that can be adopted. The courfe therein defcribed proceeds upon a dead level from the Bafon at Hereford, by Shelwicke, Wergin's Bridge, Sutton, and to the upper end of Withington's Marfh, which is fix miles to the firft Lock; from thence up the valley to Monk Hyde Green, and by Hyde Mill, to the fummit level at Canon Froome, and on to Bofbury.

I firmly believe, by taking this line, that the canal will never want water in the drieft feafons, and will be executed at a fmaller expence than in any other direction; it alfo paffes through a great deal of marfhy land, which will be drained by the canal, and confequently the country will be greatly benefitted thereby in that point of view.

I have continued the level from the tail of the lock at Bofbury road to Ledbury, whereby a Bafon may be formed within three furlongs of the Market-houfe at the top of Bye-ftreet, in that town.

Upon a careful examination of the country from Ledbury to Newent, I find it fo much interfected with hills, that it is impracticable to carry the main Line by way of Newent. But a lateral branch to Newent may be made as laid down in the plan by Mr. HALL, which, in my opinion, will anfwer every requifite purpofe.

I have made my Eftimate for a Canal of proper dimenfions for the navigation of veffels 70 feet long, and 8 feet wide, which will carry about 35 tons burthen, and draw 3 feet and 6 inches water. And I particularly recommend the ufe of thefe veffels, as they are fuch as, from my experience, I have always found to be the beft adapted for the difpatch of bufinefs on canals.

My calculation, for the execution of the plan, the particulars of which are given in my Eftimate, amounts to 69,997l. 13s. 6d.

JOSIAH CLOWES.

APRIL 27, 1790.

(1)

A N

A C T

FOR

Making and Maintaining a Navigable Canal from the City of Hereford *to the City of* Gloucester, *with a Collateral Cut from the same to the Town of* Newent *in the County of* Gloucester.

WHEREAS the making and maintaining a Navigable Preamble. Canal from or near to a Meadow called *Widemarſh,* ſituate within the Liberties of the City of *Hereford,* to communicate with the River *Severn* at or near to a Meadow called *Ox Leaſe,* ſituate within the City of *Glouceſter,* with a Collateral Cut from the ſaid Canal to the Town of *Newent* in the County of *Glouceſter,* will open a Communication with ſeveral Collieries in the Neighbourhood of *Newent* aforeſaid, and with Tracts of Land wherein are large and valuable Mines of Coal, and alſo with ſeveral Quarries of Lime-ſtone; and will likewiſe open an eaſy Communication between the County of
A *Hereford,*

The title page of the Act authoriſing the canal.

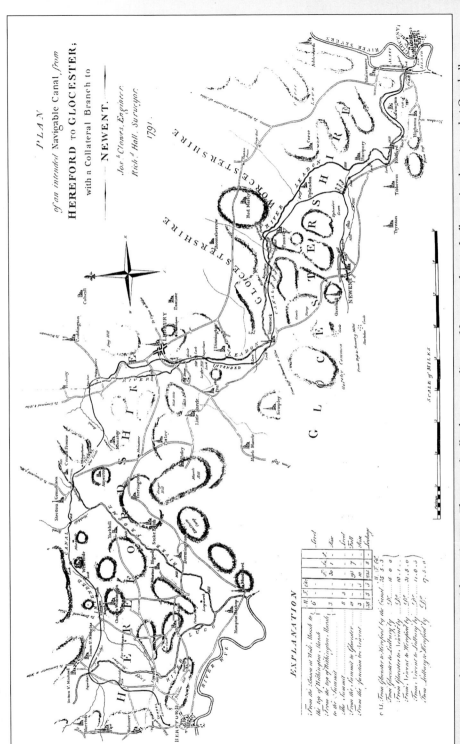

Josiah Clowes' plan of the canal, 1791. The route finally chosen ran direct to Newent and on to Ledbury via a long tunnel at Oxenhall.

shareholders, amongst whom were such well known names as Charles Brandon Trye surgeon of Gloucester, William Price timber merchant of Gloucester, Michael Hicks Beach, the Hon. Andrew Foley, John Nourse Morse of Newent, Thomas Baylis of Ledbury and R.C. Hopton of Canon Frome.

The capital was fully subscribed by the summer of 1792 and for the time being at least, the Newent coalfield had served its purpose. Hugh Henshall, Brindley's brother-in-law, was then asked to resurvey the canal and submitted plans for taking the main line by way of Newent, thus avoiding the proposed three mile branch and also in effect bringing the coalfield considerably nearer Ledbury and Hereford. The cost of the modification was likely to be a heavy one, for some very hilly country had to be crossed by a route that Clowes had already condemned as impractical. Nevertheless the revised plan was ratified by Act of Parliament in 1793. It was to prove a fatal blunder.

In keeping with the change of route, the new Act contained a number of clauses specific to mining, and coal which might be discovered during construction. In particular, mine owners employing 'fire engines' (pumping engines), if making use of the canal, were obliged to lift the water into it - a situation which may have applied for a short time at Hill House Colliery, mentioned below.

Full of optimism, the company began to develop collieries on its own account and the erection of fire engines was early considered. Success was first reported in April 1794 on the land of Mrs Phillips at Lower House where pits had been 'working with good profit' a year or two before. Sinking a shaft took five months but the coal 'not promising from its general appearance to be fit for any other purpose than lime-burning and the like', it was determined to sink another pit.

Soon afterwards, terms of one-seventh royalty were agreed with Mrs Phillips on the value of coal at surface, the small coal being worth only about three shillings per ton. By early in 1795 a seam over 6 ft thick had been reached, and a 'railroad or small collateral cut' was discussed to carry coal to the main line of canal with a possible extension westwards to limestone quarries at Gorsley, about a mile away. However the new seam proved disappointing and in May, 1795 a further pit was sunk on the land of Thomas Wood and became known as Hill House Colliery .

By November 1795 the canal company's mining speculations had lost a net £515 and an opportunity was quickly taken to hand over to Richard Perkins of Oakhill, Somerset and a friend of William Smith the geologist. As an inducement it was decided to build the already discussed branch. Perkins agreed to supply up to 4,000 tons of small coal annually for brick making and lime burning, to pay 2d. per ton for coal over the branch, also to guarantee 35 tons daily for the first three months, then 70 tons if it could be raised and sold. His first action was to dismiss all the colliers including John Webster the foreman, who had come from Nailsea in Somerset.

In June 1796 John Chadwick agreed to construct the branch by the following Michaelmas. It ran across part of the Foley estate above and parallel to an abandoned 17th century channel, constructed to bring water from pools at Gorsley to an iron blast-furnace at Newent via a large storage pond alongside

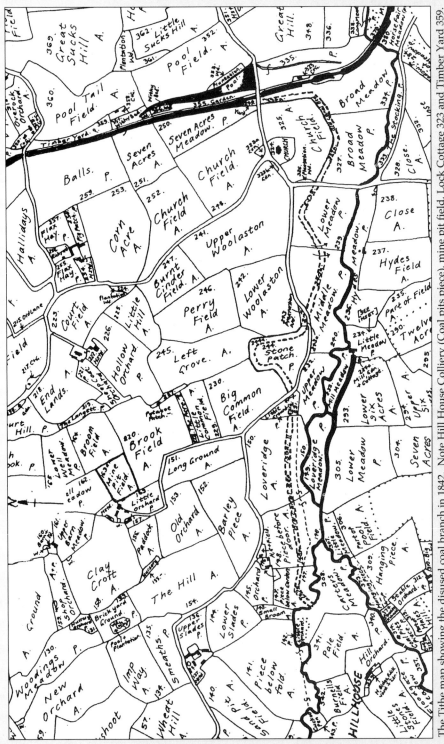

The Tithe map showing the disused coal branch in 1842. Note Hill House Colliery (Coal pits piece), mine pit field, Lock Cottage 323 and Timber Yard 359. Oxenhall tunnel is just off the map, which measures 1¼ miles in length.

Geoff Gwatkin

the canal at Oxenhall. The pond still survives, a haven for wildlife, and is often mistaken for a water supply for the canal.

A few months later the committee suspected Perkins of dragging his feet and reminded him that the branch would be ready in five weeks. 'You are under engagement to send one boat per day to market by means thereof . . . get on with sinking your new shafts as a disappointment in this instance will be big with consequences the most disagreeable to yourself and the Company.' Perkins was already about to erect a steam engine and a year afterwards became associated with John Moggridge of Boyce Court to further his commercial prospects. Moggridge (1731-1803) had been a clothier in Bradford-on-Avon before becoming Lord of the Manor of Dymock in 1794, in which year his daughter Elizabeth married Richard Perkins junior. Moggridge also had a son, John Hodder Moggridge, and the four men seem to have formed the nucleus of Perkins, Moggridge & Company.

Having strayed some distance from our main story, we must now return to the year 1793, and follow developments on the canal. By the autumn of that year there had been considerable progress, with the first 3½ miles from Over already completed and full of water. R.H. Hall was appointed surveyor and assistant to Clowes, and William Coxley of Gloucester became clerk at £100 per annum. Charles Brandon Trye was proposed for the committee and in the November it was agreed to build a feeder from Rudford Mill to the canal at Rudford lock.

At Over, the original idea of an aqueduct over the Severn had been abandoned in favour of a lock down into the river, before crossing Alney Island, where John Carne's patented earth-moving machine operated by horses was doing good work. It had previously served for two years at Pentewin Stream, St Austell, Cornwall, and it was claimed that in seven days on the canal, 'eleven men and two horses cut and removed in a very neat manner, 48 feet long, 54 feet wide and 16½ feet deep . . . upwards of 1,480 tons'. But all this effort was in the end abortive; the channel proved very liable to silting, and was soon abandoned in favour of gaining Gloucester by the Severn alone.

Carne's machine was then moved to Boyce Court, Dymock, for opening up the mouth of Oxenhall tunnel, upon which work now began in earnest.

William Maysey, who was employed as a kind of general factotum, journeyed to Sapperton tunnel on the Cotswolds, to negotiate with Samuel Smith of the Thames & Severn Canal for surplus horse gins used for shaft sinking. He acquired two gin wheels and eight pairs of small wheels for £17, which were conveyed to Oxenhall by road and canal. Quarries at Cover Street (Culver Street) Newent, and Gorsley Common supplied stone, and towards the end of 1794 three boats 50 ft long were ordered for conveying spoil from Boyce Court for embankments near Dymock. No less than six boats were proposed for a similar purpose at Canon Frome where cuttings for Ashperton or Walsopthorne tunnel were well advanced. The latter work however, virtually constituted the sum total beyond Ledbury, and amounted to little more than a token attempt to gain water essential for a successful undertaking.

Below Newent, a feeder was completed from the Tibberton Brook, and in January 1795 William Price of Gloucester laid before his fellow committee members a report upon the general state of progress. At Boyce Court, Carne's

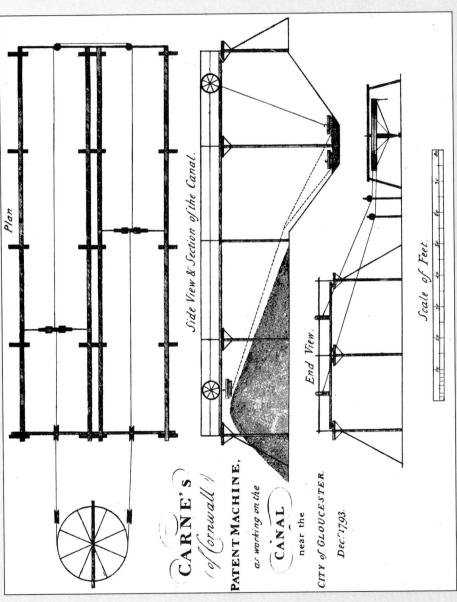

Plan

Side View & Section of the Canal.

End View.

Scale of Feet.

CARNE'S
(of Cornwall)
PATENT MACHINE,
as working on the
CANAL
near the
CITY of GLOUCESTER.
Dec.r 1793.

Carne's excavator, worked by a horse-whim as used in mining. The need to re-erect it every few yards was a considerable disadvantage.

Science Museum Library

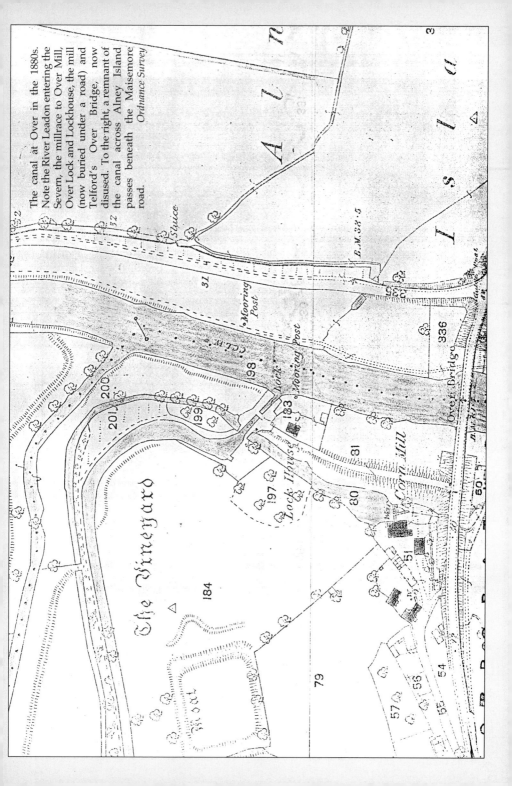

The canal at Over in the 1880s. Note the River Leadon entering the Severn, the millrace to Over Mill, Over Lock and Lockhouse, the mill (now buried under a road) and Telford's Over Bridge, now disused. To the right, a remnant of the canal across Alney Island passes beneath the Maisemore road.

Ordnance Survey

Poor investment. A hundred pound share purchased by Thomas Andrewes of Bristol.

machine 'lately improved by the addition of Cogs for the Wheels to work upon' was doing well, and various contractors were busy on the shafts and headings for the tunnel.

In 1795, Whitworth became engineer following Clowes' death at the age of only 58, and in the autumn the company's first two boats were named, the one being *Dean Tucker*, after the Dean of Gloucester, and the other, *Newent Trader*. The latter was scheduled to leave Newent at 4 pm on Friday 20th November, and to reach Gloucester next day in time for the market, after spending the night at Rudford. But even this simple expedition went wrong. The boat arrived too late due to the frost 'and the unskilfulness of Thomas Weston', though exactly what happened is uncertain. It was an ominous portent.

By the winter of 1795 the works were falling badly behind. At the tunnel at least 20 shafts and probably as many as 24 were sunk, with water and spoil raised in barrels by gins and windlasses; the task proved excessively strenuous for both horses and men, no less than 60 barrels per hour being wound from one shaft alone. Tunnel builders always dreaded encountering springs, and frantic attempts were made to drive communications between adjacent shafts and through to either end. Drilled by hand and blasted by gunpowder, the headings measured only 3 ft square and conditions must have been appalling. Errors in heights compounded the difficulties, and in July 1796 the committee found itself with no alternative but to adopt steam power. It was determined to install:

> . . . two Fire Engines, one on the 9th Pit South end, and one on the 11th Pit at the North end, Ordered. That application be made to the Coalbrook Dale Company, Mr William Reynolds, Mr Bull, Mr John Winwood and Mr John Curr to know their respective prices of erecting a Fire Engine, including Pump, Cylinders, and every other apparatus, to draw at the depth of 50 yards, 2,000, 2,500 and 3,000 Gallons of Water an Hour . . .

A month later Coalbrookdale and John Curr received orders for one engine each, to be erected as soon as possible.

At the November General Meeting the shareholders were informed of the company's predicament and a gloomier picture could hardly have been conceived. For the expenditure of almost £100,000 - more than Clowes' original estimate for the whole line - the halfway town of Ledbury was still out of sight and as for the coalfield, the committee could only report that Mr Perkins' mine 'justifies the sanguine hopes long entertained by your committee that it will be ultimately productive of great pecuniary advantages to your undertaking '.

Net revenue due to tonnage to Newent amounted to a derisory £95, the low figure being attributed in the main to a reluctance of farmers and tradesmen to adopt the new mode of transport. Another disaster was at Oxenhall where:

> Great has been the delay and expence, which your Committee has been obliged to witness, in the progress of the tunnel, and which have arisen from the immense quantity of water, issuing in the course of the works, which has several times filled pits only half sunk, and driven the workmen entirely from their labour. Extraordinary exertions have been used to discharge the water, but in many instances without effect. These circumstances have induced the Committee at length to determine on the erection of two steam engines, as the only certain means of carrying on the work with proper expedition, and consequently of completing it in any definite time.

The Coalbrookdale engine was desperately needed at shaft No. 7, and early in 1797 Mr Curr's engine was lying in pieces for want of a man to erect it. Only a few weeks later, it was dismantled even before its assembly had been finished at the north end, in order to meet some greater emergency at No. 9 shaft. Somehow the work was eventually finished, but a legacy of the chaos forever remained in the crooked and tortuous bore through which daylight could never be seen. Years later, Stephen Ballard, the canal engineer, recorded that after obtaining considerable sums in advance for work on the tunnel, many contractors had decamped without fulfilling their contract, much to the general mortification. In short, we cannot help but feel that much of the company's troubles were borne of sheer lack of business acumen and experience, thus compounding the folly of the Newent route.

As to the question of finishing the canal to Hereford, Whitworth estimated the need for a further £70,000, a figure which was rightly described as 'certainly enormous when added to that already expended'. But the difficulties were further compounded because from the beginning, the rivers Frome or Lodon, well beyond Ledbury, were to have provided the chief source of water without

A culvert on the coal branch in 1976. The Gloucester-Ledbury railway was on the left; note the bridge in the background. *Author*

Taken in the 1960s, this picture reveals the state of Oxenhall tunnel where it passes through the coal measures. *Alan Simpson*

which not even opening to that town would enable trade of the district fully to develop. Nevertheless, Ledbury was an essential goal if hope of some return might be entertained. Efforts therefore concentrated upon the tunnel of which one-third was still unwrought, and £4,000 was raised for opening to a wharf on the Ross-Ledbury road a mile short of the town. Work now proceeded rapidly, and the official opening took place on 29th March, 1798.

> We have the satisfaction to announce to the Public [reported the *Gloucester Journal*] that the Herefordshire & Gloucestershire Canal is completed as far as Ledbury. The opening took place on Friday last, on which day several of the Proprietors and Gentlemen of the Committee embarked at the junction of the Coal Branch near Newent, in the first vessel laden with merchandize which was followed by three others laden with Coal. They passed through the Tunnel at Oxenhall which is 2,192 yards in length in 52 minutes; at the farther end they were met by several Gentlemen and entertained with a cold collation at the Boyce, the seat of Mr Moggeridge.
> Both ends of the Tunnel, as well as the several Bridges on the Canal, were lined with spectators, who hailed the boats with reiterated acclamations; indeed the sight was very impressive, and it is supposed that upwards of 2,000 people were present on their arrival at Ledbury . . .

The benefits to the neighbourhood were immediate since best quality coal was now on sale at 13*s*. 6*d*. per ton instead of 24*s*. But whether this valuable commodity had derived from Newent is doubtful, for although the collieries had expanded to a certain extent, an inferior product was still largely limiting demand to brick making and lime burning. In the latter capacity Perkins had already applied for permission to erect kilns at Newent and at the junction of the colliery branch, and to acquire three of the canal company's boats at £60 each. Some revenue accrued, for Perkins Moggridge & Co. agreed to pay ½*d*. per ton wharfage on all coal and limestone deposited on wharves at Newent, Dymock and Ledbury for as long as their interests in Mr Foley's and other collieries endured. Unfortunately the resulting traffic created its own problems, the partners being shortly afterwards accused of damaging the tunnel with square-ended boats without rudders.

This, however, did not dissuade Perkins from requesting 'to make an opening in the form of a circular arch 5 ft diameter through one of the side walls of the tunnel with the view of making some trial for coal discovered there'. In spite of precedents elsewhere, consent was refused as 'it appears to the committee to be impossible to work any mine by means thereof without greatly impending the navigation'. But by this time it seems that Perkins Moggridge & Co. were diverting their attention to the Gorsley quarries, where a battery of kilns was constructed, and by the end of 1799 the committee sadly recorded that in spite of considerable production very little coal was actually passing along the canal. Some did reach destinations as far afield as clothiers' works on the Stroudwater Canal, but before long the colliery branch fell into disuse and the mines into oblivion, at least so far as the canal was concerned.

In fact, the canal, far from enhancing the coalfield's potential, such as it was, in great measure destroyed it by importing better coal via the Severn. Nonetheless, the vision lingered; the company clung to the branch for another 40 years after abandonment, being 'unwilling to give up the power of a communication so long as there is any prospect of a good bed of coal being discovered'. Further details of this intriguing little coalfield are given in my *Mines of Newent & Ross*, 1987, and according to Michael Handford, writing in to me in 1982, 'the complete business records of Perkins, Moggridge & Perkins . . . that would about fill a tea-chest altogether', had come to light and were in his possession. Let us hope their contents will one day be revealed.

Before finally leaving the coal canal, one might have supposed its potential as a source of much-needed water would have justified its retention. At Gorsley were three big storage ponds, ex-Newent Ironworks, just waiting to feed into the branch at Hill House Colliery. But in spite of talk as early as 1799, it was never done.

The grand concept of an inland navigation from Gloucester to Hereford was thus diminished to a 16 mile ribbon of water serving a few villages and a couple of small market towns with little enough industry in any form. Nonetheless, in hopes that revenue might be made to exceed operating costs, trade was developed as far as possible, William Maysey being appointed manager at Ledbury for the minimal salary of £30 per annum. Maintaining an adequate supply of water was the first requirement, and in August 1798 he was ordered to use 'every exertion to complete the Steam Engine and feeder at and from the Leather Mill to Ledbury Pound . . .' The engine may have derived from Oxenhall tunnel, but it does not appear to have remained in use for very long. In March 1798 it was agreed to dispose of the larger Oxenhall engine to Messrs Vaughan & Co. for £227, but all further trace is lost.

Before the end of the year Maysey found himself in serious trouble for insolent behaviour. He was dismissed, but regained his job 'on expressing his deep regret and determination to pay strict attention to the order of the committee in future'. Incidents such as this were hardly surprising, for the venture had exhausted the spirit of all concerned. The money expended (£104,000) had far exceeded the estimate for the whole distance and with the euphoria of the canal mania already past, very few were the numbers ready to enthuse over the prospect of completion, even if it might have been had for nothing.

Chapter Three

A Renaissance

In the early part of the 19th century, the affairs of the Herefordshire & Gloucestershire Canal Navigation Company is shrouded in darkness. The problems of obtaining a quorum precluded a single meeting of shareholders or management committee for more than a decade, for in the words of Charles Hadfield it was 'difficult to induce the proprietors to take an interest in a canal which appeared unlikely ever to yield them a penny'.

Information on trade at this period is scanty, but one type of traffic was building stone for Eastnor Castle near Ledbury, designed by Robert Smirke, and begun in 1812. In addition, there would doubtless have been the novelty of stone water-pipes machined out of the solid, examples of which may still be encountered in the area. These pipes were manufactured on a huge scale at Guiting on the Cotswolds, brought by road to Cheltenham and thence over the newly-opened tramroad to Gloucester. Transhipment to barges would then have conveyed them to either Newent or Ledbury and finally by road to their destination. A century later, these pipes were discovered and described in a learned journal as Roman! Details of this remarkable enterprise are given in my *The Gloucester & Cheltenham Tramroad*, Oakwood Press, 1987.

Signs of a revival did not occur until November 1812, when William Price and John Biddulph of Ledbury Park numbered amongst those elected to form a committee. Biddulph (1768-1845), whose family had connections with the Middeltons of Chirk Castle, was a man of wide experience who had sailed as second mate on a trading ship to India. He was also a partner in Cocks & Biddulph, bankers of Charing Cross, and well versed in mining and industry generally. Furthermore, the canal crossed his land, and his desire to improve trade and commerce proved of much assistance to the undertaking. As for the company's few servants, their loyal efforts during the intervening years were manifest when William Maysey announced £1,200 in credit, enabling plans to be laid for construction of a reservoir and repair of three fish-ponds near Ledbury for the same purpose.

Early in 1818, the committee resolved to build a wharf and a house for the clerk at Over where the canal started, the house being ready by the end of the year. It seems, however, that these developments were not at the junction with the river, but some distance away, for in 1829 we learn that a new house and wharf were to be built at Over lock. The house was completed in 1831, with 'three rooms up, two down, back kitchen, pump, oven, warehouse, stable, and every convenience'.

When in August 1827, shareholders at last managed to convene a further meeting, considerable progress had been made. The canal had by now achieved a relatively stable position, with trade improved as far as a shortage of water and inhibiting effects of a turnpike toll between the terminus and Ledbury would allow. Profits in proportion to invested capital were still too trivial to permit a dividend, but nonetheless the venture was again receiving attention, as

25

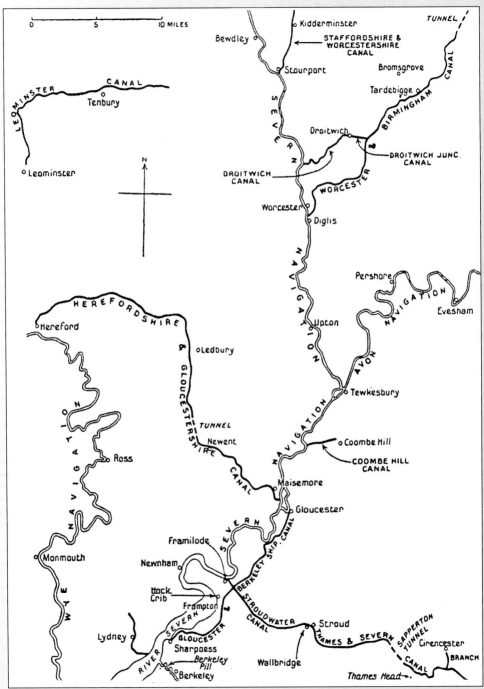

The canal in relation to other waterways, reproduced from Charles Hadfield's *British Canals*, 5th edition.

can be inferred from the new committee appointed. John Biddulph took the chair, and others included his son Robert, Earl Somers of Eastnor Castle, Thomas Ballard and James Kyrle Money - all men of substance residing within a mile or two of the town. Such an interest had to be local or it was nothing, for where else might concern be expressed in a half-formed waterway in the depths of rural England?

An important task was to appoint a successor to William Maysey who was retiring. The choice fell upon a young man of 23 years from Malvern Link named Stephen Ballard, and there is hardly a doubt that John Biddulph was his sponsor, for the banker was well acquainted with the Baylis family of whom Ballard's mother Charlotte was a member. Stephen Ballard's sole experience relating to business and engineering amounted to horticulture, and a couple of years' apprenticeship to Henry Lucy, a builder of Cheltenham. Lucy later became manager of the Gloucester & Cheltenham tramroad, and Ballard never forgot his old master, often putting business in his path.

It speaks well for Biddulph's judgement that a better man could not have been found, and in spite of a great difference in their ages (Biddulph was nearly 60) the two were able to provide the commercial acumen, ability and drive essential for developments that were to follow.

One of Ballard's first challenges was the very deep lock at Over, a constant source of trouble throughout the canal's life. Amongst other problems, it created a heavy drain on water, especially after the passage of several boats when the river was low. By agreement with Sir William Guise, the answer was to empty the top half of the lock into the pond of Over Mill (now beneath the new road), and to fill the lower half from the same pool - a very ingenious solution. 'That a work of such importance at so trifling an expense remained so long undone is astonishing', wrote Ballard.

Soon after his appointment, Ballard put forward a plan which although ostensibly to bring water from the River Frome, in reality formed a first step in a more ambitious project since the feeder, suitably enlarged, could form the first seven miles of a canal to Hereford.

In July 1828, Robert Stephenson, then only 24 years old, surveyed the intended watercourse and afterwards dined at Ledbury Park in some style. The main course included 'a haunch of 4 year old venison very good flavored, and weighed 22 lb', recorded John Biddulph. But the older man was not convinced about the wisdom of extending to the city, at least by canal. It seemed to him its time had gone. The Stephensons, were of course, pro-railway, and in addition, the Hereford-Abergavenny tramroad had opened only a week or two before. But the local feeling was too entrenched against new-fangled ideas to pay much attention, though the spectre of railways was to arise time and time again.

Ballard submitted his case in a booklet with the following estimate of the cost of getting to Hereford:

BOYCE BRIDGE
DYMOCK "32

An old postcard scene of the bridge at Boyce Court, just north of Oxenhall tunnel, where
the canal still retains its water.

	£
Purchase of 17 miles of land, each mile containing 5 Acres, at £70 per acre	5,950
Allow for damage of land ¼ of the above	1,487
Excavating 17 miles, at 3s. per yard running	4,488
Allow the same sum reducing inequalities	4,488
Eight Locks, at £700 each	5,600
Seventeen arch bridges, at £80 each	1,360
Twenty-five wood bridges, at £30 each	750
Culverts and aqueducts	3,000
Puddling, at 8d. per yard, running the whole distance	997
Towing path, gates, fences	1,880
	£30,000

Bearing in mind the cost of building to Ledbury in the 1790s, Ballard must have known such a figure was quite inadequate, for when he put a detailed report to the committee in September 1829, it had risen to £52,958. In the end, even this fell short, for promoters as a whole are not only optimists, but also very wary of pricing their dreams out of court. Hence the golden rule ever applies, that the true cost at least doubles, and no better example can be found than the Channel Tunnel.

But to return to the canal. Ballard's 1829 report provided for the accommodation of boats 70 ft long and 8 ft beam, and assumed a channel of generous proportions, being 27 ft wide at the top and 6 ft deep instead of the earlier 4½ ft. The extra depth was to provide a reserve of water, deter weeds and to create less drag on the boats. Slight changes in the old plans were also included, with long cuttings instead of tunnels at Ashperton and Aylestone near Hereford. The extra annual revenue he estimated at £4,750, and based on such a sum the case looked attractive, Ballard concluded the report with the words:

> On my first entering on the business of this canal I was led to believe that there was no trade for a canal, that even the short time in each year that it was navigable was sufficient for the trade, and that if there was ever so good a supply of water the trade would not be increased thereby.
> The erroneousness of this opinion was proved by the tonnage receipts in the year 1828 . . . Ever since I have been in your employ I have applied myself to the consideration of the completion of the canal and the study of canals in general. The more I become acquainted with the subject the more desirable to the company and the country at large does completion of this appear to me . . .

Ballard was clearly the mainspring behind the new enthusiasm, and as for the committee, perhaps faith in the man exceeded their better judgement. At all events, none would wish to voice a doubt when for the first time in over 30 years optimism was in the air.

Thus, in the twilight of the canal age, was cast the die that moulded the last main-line navigation in the southern half of England.

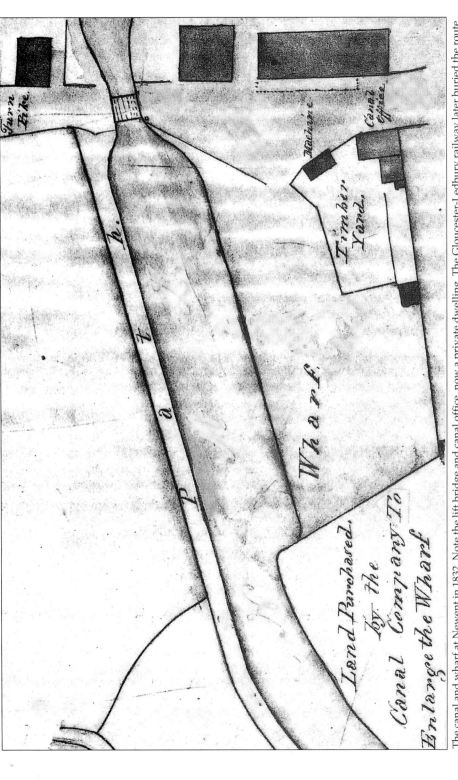

Turn Pike.

Wharf.

Warehouse

Canal Office.

Timber Yard.

Land Purchased by the Canal Company To Enlarge the Wharf

The canal and wharf at Newent in 1832. Note the lift bridge and canal office, now a private dwelling. The Gloucester-Ledbury railway later buried the route, see the plan on page 101.　　GRO

Chapter Four

Stephen Ballard's Canal

In a small way, a start had already been made by doubling the size of the basin at Ledbury Wharf by incorporating an old moat alongside, but for the time being little more could be done beyond building a lock through which the first boat passed on 20th May, 1832. Ballard was now described as 'clerk and engineer' at a salary of £150 per annum.

Increasing trade had justified warehouses and weighbridges at Newent and Ledbury, whilst at the latter, improvements also included a carpenter's shop, a stable and a shed for drying timber. In addition, the company now owned various boats, one being a small vessel kept in the Severn to help barges in the tricky manoeuvre of getting into Over lock. The canal however, was still about a mile short of Ledbury town centre, several more locks being needed for the climb up to Bye Street.

We must now turn to events elsewhere, for the recently opened Gloucester & Berkeley Canal was still heavily in debt after incurring an almost ruinous cost of construction. The money for completion had come largely from the Exchequer Loan Commission, who were now much in need of any means of increasing traffic to counter an outstanding debt of some £200,000. It was anticipated that completion of the Hereford & Gloucester Canal would attract Bristol-Hereford goods over the Berkeley, and in October 1834 with this incentive in mind Ballard and Biddulph approached the Exchequer Loan Office for funds.

Meanwhile, Ballard had surveyed a revised route to Hereford deviating from the Parliamentary line at Ashperton and following the Frome to the River Wye below the city. Such a plan, drawn up in May 1835, sought to avoid a lengthy embankment over the Lugg valley and a tunnel under Aylestone Hill. Before review of a loan could be made the Commissioners requested an authorising Act to sanction the deviation and also to raise capital for the project.

While the matter was under consideration a railway put forward in 1836 from Gloucester to Hereford via Ross or Ledbury provided the inklings of a new and insidious form of competition. A well attended meeting took place at Hereford on 5th October, 1836 to consider a report submitted by I.K. Brunel on the best route for such a line, and a little later a similar spectre appeared in the form of the England & Ireland Union Railway via Newent.

Although both subjects foundered, every member of committee must have recalled with apprehension that coming events cast their shadows before them. With railways advancing in all parts of the country the canal age was verging on decline, and an extension to Hereford could no longer bear a truly critical examination. But now that the ambitions of many years were within sight of realization, cold logic was not and could not be applied; the contemplation of losing all that had been striven for was too much to bear. Nevertheless, the company was hard-headed enough to appreciate the chance of quick profit from a route capable of conversion to the new mode of transport, and the possibility was constantly borne in mind as a means of underwriting the risk.

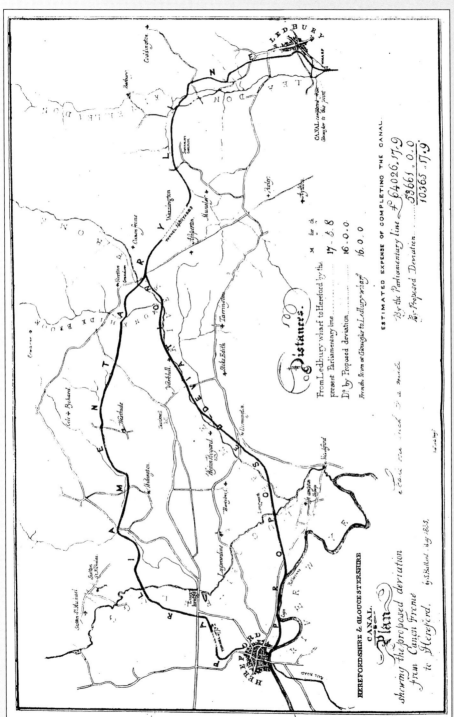

Ballard's plan of May, 1835, with his proposed deviation from Canon Frome to Hereford. In 1838 he put forward another alternative as shown on page 34. Note the Hereford-Abergavenny Tramroad, extreme left.

HRC

The proposals therefore proceeded without delay, and during the winter of 1837 and much of 1838 Ballard was largely occupied in preparing surveys and plans including the possibility of a link-up with the Leominster Canal, and a deviation down the River Lugg as an alternative to the Frome Valley.

The three options under review for the route between Canon Frome and Hereford he put before the shareholders in a report dated 13th June, 1838, were as follows:

1. The old Parliamentary line via Withington and a tunnel under Aylestone Hill.
2. Down the Frome Valley as proposed in 1835, but entering the Wye at Rotherwas rather than close to the city itself. This would save the tunnel and some 3 miles of canal but entailed a weir and lock in the river at Eign. But it would also open up trade on the river as far as its limitations allowed, as well as providing direct access to wharves and warehouses at Hereford, and the Abergavenny Tramroad. 'The advantages would be very great', wrote Ballard.
3. Following the Parliamentary line, then south down the Lugg Valley into the Wye at Rotherwas, as in option 2.

Ballard described the second option as 'undoubtedly the best', if Hereford and the Wye were the only objectives. But they were not, at least in his eyes. The old vision of a link with Leominster still lingered, to the extent that he finally recommended option 3, which would have materially aided such a development. No mention however, was made of the likely cost of the link, which would merely have proved another millstone in the company's affairs. A century and a half later, it is worth observing that had either of these deviations been adopted, the task of the Herefordshire & Gloucestershire Canal Trust in re-opening the whole canal would have been made considerably less onerous, not of course that such an eventuality would have crossed Ballard's mind for an instant. Some 20 years later, in the name of progress, he had no qualms in sacrificing the child of his own begetting on the altar of modern railways.

In the end, Ballard's preference was over-ruled, perhaps because of the cost and delay in a new Bill for an amended route. The civil engineer James Walker was requested to examine the plans and estimates, and on 29th September, 1838 both men walked over hill, hedge and ditch from Prior's Court to Hereford, where the night was spent at the Green Dragon. Whether they followed the Parliamentary line only is not clear, but at all events the long trek had not tired Ballard. Although next day was a Sunday, '8 o'clock and Mr Walker not yet up', he complained. Walker quickly came to a decision and advised adherence to the old route, albeit with slight amendments suggested by Ballard or himself. One of them advocated a considerably shortened tunnel at Ashperton by means of longer and deeper approach cuttings, an economy which in the end gave rise to a full quota of anxiety and trouble.

There was henceforth much activity. Plans were to be deposited by the end of November and a Gloucester surveyor, Arthur Causton, was engaged to undertake the work. The task finished on time but the results did not impress Stephen Ballard, who recorded that Causton's assistants were a lot of boys who could not be relied upon.

The necessary Act to complete the canal passed the House of Lords unopposed in May 1839, enabling £50,000 to be raised by mortgage and £45,000

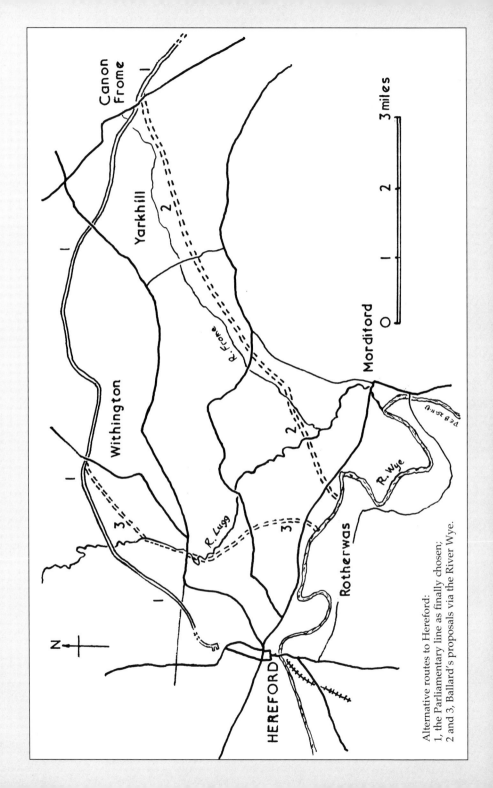

Alternative routes to Hereford:
1, the Parliamentary line as finally chosen;
2 and 3, Ballard's proposals via the River Wye.

by shares. Three months later the company's office in Homend Street, Ledbury, issued a rosy Prospectus entitled 'Completion of the Herefordshire & Gloucestershire Canal'. The cost was now estimated at £76,000 but the anticipated total income had risen to £16,125, nearly four times Ballard's estimate of 1829 and almost 10 times its current revenue.
The figures comprised as follows:

Imports and Exports of Hereford:

	£.	s.	d.
Timber, corn, cider, poles, lath, hurdles, fruits, hops, wood, charcoal, salt, slate, tiles, deals, and other building materials, & c. 23,500 tons, at 2d. per ton per mile	6,658	6	8
Coal, 10,000 tons, at 2s. 6d.per ton	1,250	0	0
Goods now carried by common stage waggons, and by barges on the River Wye, viz. sugar and other articles of grocery, iron and iron mongery goods, Manchester goods, furniture, pottery glass, cheese, & c. 4,000 tons, at 2d. per ton mile	1,133	6	8

Imports and Exports of the Country between Ledbury and Hereford:

	£.	s.	d.
Articles of the same kind as mentioned above, 20000 tons, at 2d. per ton mile for the average distance	4,083	6	8
Income of the Canal between Ledbury and Gloucester at present, £1700: with a regular supply of water this income will increase to, at least	3,000	0	0
Total income	16,125	0	0

In case this enticement proved insufficient, the Prospectus foresaw the potential of very considerable income from trade with neighbouring towns, the dream of an extension north being once more resurrected for the purpose.

There is no doubt that a water-communication, from the Leominster Canal, with the Herefordshire and Gloucestershire Canal, will speedily follow its completion to Hereford. A survey has been made, which proves that this communication (by means of a navigation about twelve miles long) may be effected at a trifling expense. A navigation uniting these two Canals would, at the lowest calculation, produce an addition to the revenue of the Shareholders in the Herefordshire and Gloucestershire Canal of at least £8,000.
That a water-communication would be formed with the town of Bromyard (situated about seven miles from the line of the Canal) is very probable, a cursory survey showing that there are no apparent difficulties. If such a communication were effected, another source of a considerable additional revenue would be opened to the Company.

To raise the £45,000 share capital, 2,250 preference shares at £20 were to be issued, and purchasers would receive 7½ per cent out of the revenue of the canal from the commencement of paying calls. Ballard bought 29, though not all at once.
The committee now comprised 18 in number, at least 10 of whom were resident in the vicinity of Ledbury - Earl Somers (Eastnor), Major-General Sir James Kyrle Money, Revd K.E. Money (Much Birch), John and Robert Biddulph, Captain George Watson (Bronsil) and four Ledbury men, T. Spencer, Thomas Ballard, Hubert Edy an attorney, and old Thomas Baylis, who was known as

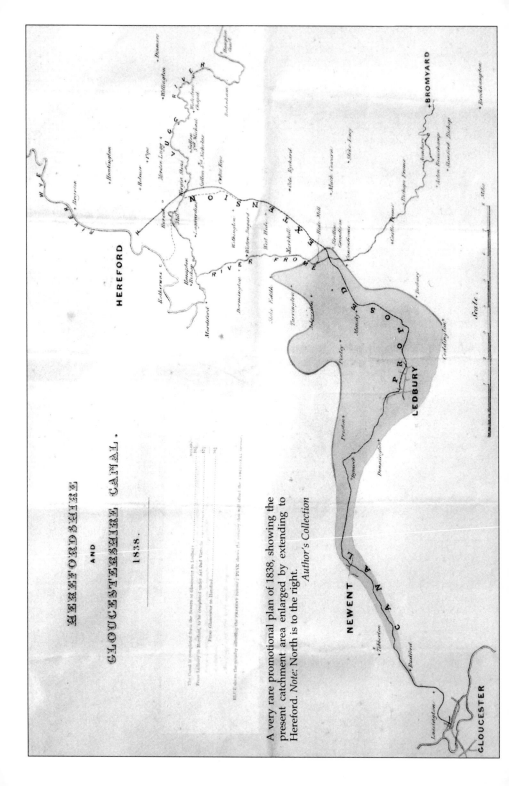

HEREFORDSHIRE

AND

GLOUCESTERSHIRE CANAL.

1838.

A very rare promotional plan of 1838, showing the present catchment area enlarged by extending to Hereford. *Note*: North is to the right.

Author's Collection

'the father of the canal'. Others included E.T. Foley MP, Archdeacon Onslow of Newent, William Washbourne and Samuel Baker of Gloucester. The whole enterprise had more in common with a family business than a large commercial undertaking, and in fact the four Ledbury men were all interrelated by marriage.

£18,000 had been subscribed as early as December 1838, and in the following June the company purchased 400,000 bricks from Stephen's brother Robert, who had a brickyard near the town.

In the autumn of 1839 Ballard was fully occupied in pegging out the line of canal and dealing with landowners. Excavation commenced on 17th November. 'The first I saw of the workmen was through a gap in the hedge', he wrote, 'and I must say the appearance of them had an electrical effect on me, never shall I forget it'. He spent much time with his brother Philip checking the 1838 survey as far as the River Frome 'as it is of such vital importance'. A discrepancy of only .05 ft was discovered, but 'in totting up my level book made the mistake of six feet. This alarmed me much when I considered what the consequences would be'.

A temporary 'rail-road' was laid down for conveying spoil, and Ballard designed a special tail-board to allow wagons to discharge without stopping. By April 1840, 500 men were engaged at Prior's Court embankment, Swinmore and elsewhere, and a 300 yd plateway was laid to convey materials at Ledbury.

Ballard was now employed fully 16 hours a day. 'Commenced work on the canal soon after 4 am' he recorded on 29th May, 'was tired by breakfast time but was hard at it till nine pm'. S. Willcox (his apprentice) was so tired that he had to remain at Ashperton. A fortnight later Ballard 'drove with S. Willcox at 5 am to Ashperton where we commenced measuring towards Ledbury where we arrived at 6 pm'. As if the day's work had not been enough, he returned the same evening for a quiet survey after the men had left. 'This I think is a good plan, as my attention is not distracted from taking a general view.'

On 22nd February, 1841 the first load of coal arrived at Bye Street, Ledbury, where the new lock-gates were on Ballard's principle, being constructed wholly of timber devoid of ironwork as a means of preventing rot. The rise through the five locks from the Ross Road was some 60 ft. The canal was now almost completed as far as Prior's Court and work had begun on shafts for the excavation of Ashperton tunnel, 400 yds long. Its shortened length however, was to prove a doubtful economy, demanding much longer and deeper cuttings than those begun in the 1790s. Gunpowder was needed to remove heavy marl formations, but some excellent beds of stone proved useful for construction work.

Nearby, Ballard had a temporary home built of dry bricks with only a few courses of mortar, and into this strange abode he moved on 21st August, 1841. Much trouble was experienced in keeping the shafts clear of water, with men and horses sometimes working round the clock, and one night Ballard stayed up until 1 am with a boy who had fallen 60 ft down a shaft. The whole tunnel was potentially unstable, necessitating lining throughout with brick and stone, and on one occasion the timber centring was subjected to excessive strain by a run of ground extending right up to surface.

The very tight bridge at Withington with the Lock-keeper's house beyond. The stone tablet over the arch is dated 1843. *Author*

In addition to engineering worries, Ballard was heavily occupied with as many as 54 landowners between Canon Frome and Hereford, most of whom drove the hardest possible bargain. John Homes of Stretton Grandison took the company to court over four acres of land where the embankment crossed the Frome Valley. Settlement was made without reference to the company's offer to provide accommodation culverts and bridges, and amounted to £2,000 - a very high sum in those days. Ballard was 'much disgusted and disheartened with this decision'.

Although from the earliest days a water supply from the River Frome was vital to the Hereford extension, it was not legally established until November 1841. The company agreed to pay John Hopton of Canon Frome Court £1,050 for an absolute right to all the water that flowed over a weir to be built for the purpose.

In the early part of 1842, the feeder from this weir provided the chief pre-occupation. The river was tapped just above Canon Frome Court, the residence of John Hopton and his family, and conveyed through the grounds to the canal by a cut-and-cover brick culvert 4 ft 2 in. high and 3 ft 4 in. wide, up to 16 ft deep and over half a mile in length. The work was completed in two months. The waters of the Frome were let into the canal on 20th August, when it was nearly empty the whole way to Gloucester. To celebrate the achievement of half a century's aspirations, two barrels of cider were provided for the navvies, and a drunken orgy followed in the tunnel which greatly displeased the committee and the tee-total Ballard.

At this time, earth was being punted down the canal for construction of the Frome embankment, and the tunnel approaches during an exceptionally wet season created much anxiety. On 27th August a terrible slip took place which needed immediate removal to maintain the flow of water towards Ledbury. A little later nearly 2 inches of rain fell in 18 hours, leading to more trouble. 'The committee not in very good spirits' recorded Ballard, 'the slips are so disheartening and we have not much money in hand'. Progress was now considerably retarded, and on 24th September, 1842 he had to admit that his estimates had been exceeded. Nevertheless, a few days later John Biddulph generously recommended a holiday, but Ballard 'declined on account of the fear of the company's interest suffering in my absence'. He was in fact very low in spirits, still suffering from the frequent and severe headaches that had plagued him for years, and anxious for his father who was gravely ill; he died a few weeks later. On November 2nd, Ballard moved to a dwelling at Canon Frome called 'The Nutshell', and next day his 'late residence at the tunnel', a somewhat grandiose title for the house of bricks, was pulled down.

Incessant bad weather continued to cause anxiety. 'Still raining heavily', wrote Ballard, 'much afraid it would start our slips again, so slept in chair by fire all night and went out very early , much pleased to find no great mischief'. The following day he went to Birmingham, arriving at midnight, in an effort to borrow £13,000. He returned empty-handed on the recently-opened Birmingham & Gloucester Railway and 'was much pleased with the regularity and comfort of railway travelling'. After snatching a few hours sleep in Tewkesbury, he caught the 3.30 am mail coach to Ledbury, involving a long

The middle of the three canal basins at Hereford, from an old print. See also the two more recent photographs on page 84.

HEREFORD WHARF.

26 Febry 1840

Weighed on the

HEREFORD and GLOUCESTER

Canal Weighing Machine.

By *H Harbour*,

COAL, from *R Whitehouse*

To *M Lawrence*

Tons.	C.	Q.
1	0	0

climb hard against the collars over the Hollybush Pass, that took no less than 2½ hours for the 14 miles. Schedules such as this were typical of an engineer's life in those days.

Shortage of cash and hard bargains with greedy landowners had by now almost exhausted resources, and for the present little hope could be entertained of extending further. Nonetheless, substantial progress had been made. 'On Wednesday last' reported the *Hereford Journal* of 11th January, 1843, 'the spirited carriers Messers Bunning and Gibson had their first boatload of goods to Canon Frome Wharf. From that day may be dated the desertion of the river Wye as a navigation for the conveyance of foreign produce . . .' A week later Ballard moved into a new house at the wharf which was alongside the main road at the end of Ashperton village.

Brisk development of trade soon attracted capital, £13,000 being in the bank by 8th May, and a weekly passenger boat to Ledbury market was well patronized. By midsummer construction to Withington was in full swing. The Frome embankment was described as 'a very long and hard piece of work', but a further difficulty arose at Monkhide. Although Causton's plan of 1838 had indicated a course bypassing the village on the north side, for some reason a more southerly line was adopted in spite of intervening roads. One of these intersected the route at a very sharp angle, but instead of building a conventional bridge at right angles, or even deflecting the canal itself, a magnificent skew construction was erected at an obliquity exceeding 60° to enable the road alignment to be maintained. Indeed, there is hardly an example on the whole extension where a road, however minor, was deviated to simplify a bridge.

The Monkhide instance was however, exceptional, and we are tempted to suspect that the reason behind this little gem of civil engineering was nothing more than Ballard indulging in a display of technical virtuosity. Certainly this element must have presided to some extent, and the inner satisfaction that it gave him would not have been lessened by its situation, unknown and unappreciated except by bargemen and country folk in this secluded backwater of Herefordshire .

Ballard had drawn up plans for the bridge as early as January 1839 but although construction appears to have gone smoothly enough, misgivings arose when the time came to remove the centring. 'There were so many props we could not let down the arch regularly, only a part at a time, this caused cracks which much alarmed me, and I stayed with it as long as I could see and felt very anxious about it'. Next day, Sunday 3rd December, he went again to the spot still very concerned, and on the Monday 'went to direct the men how to balance it, lightened one part and loaded the other'. More cracks appeared on removal of further centring but eventually he seemed satisfied with the outcome.

In February 1844 the canal opened to Withington wharf, almost within sight of Hereford. This important event was marked by the arrival of two packet-boats full of shareholders and well-wishers from Ledbury, and augmented by no less than 27 working boats laden with coal and merchandize. The convoy arrived to the tumultuous welcome of 3,000 spectators and afterwards Ballard, the committee and various dignitaries journeyed to a dinner at the City Arms,

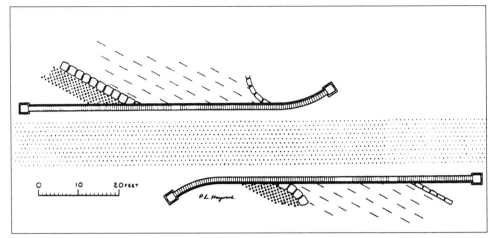

Ballard's masterpiece. 'Skew bridge continues to stand well' he wrote on 23rd November 1843. The canal has recently been restored in this vicinity.

Below and opposite: Views of the bridge looking in oppisite directions. *(Both) Author's Collection*

Hereford. It speaks volumes for the esteem to which he was held, and to the tact and diplomacy which he had exercised, that the sponsors were the very landowners who had given rise to so many difficult encounters over the preceding years. But whilst the numerous toasts revealed a great determination to complete the venture, it was also apparent that the city inhabitants were hardly extending their enthusiasm as far as their pockets. Very few shares had been taken up in the vicinity, indeed, far more capital had come from Birmingham. One investor was Charles Bulmer, a wine merchant of Hereford, and somehow sufficient funds accrued from other sources to continue.

Ballard now moved to Withington and by January 1845 work along the last stretch of canal was going well. The ¼ mile of tunnel under Aylestone Hill proceeded rapidly, 63 yards being excavated in a fortnight, but in other respects prospects were far from satisfactory. There were difficulties in paying interest on mortgages and in March 1845 the committee resolved to attempt a sell-out to the Great Western Railway.

Ballard was now very depressed about 'the bad prospects that surround our canal. Railways everywhere and no funds to complete our little work without personal security'. Overspent and in debt, the venture bore haunting resemblance to its state on gaining Ledbury nearly half a century before. But this time, no doubt sensing an almost total apathy on the part of the public, the company arranged no celebrations and not a single person came out of the city to witness the filling of the basin on 22nd May, 1845. The *Hereford Times* devoted less space to the occasion than to the latest state of the fatstock market, for it was now the hour of the Railway Mania.

On the same day Stephen Ballard left Withington for a new appointment in the Fens. 'The country looked beautiful' he wrote, 'and I could not refrain from shedding tears, near 18 years have I been employed on the canal and my spirits dropped when the hour arrived'. Firmly though his reputation as an engineer had been established, the memory of that morning in spring must have lingered within him for the remainder of his days.

The Lugg aqueduct in 1922, and long since demolished. The central arch bears the date 1844.   *R&CHS*

Chapter Five

A Falling Star

Having at last achieved its goal, the Herefordshire & Gloucestershire Canal Navigation Company again experienced great difficulties in obtaining a quorum. Costs of the extension had been heavy, amounting to £141,436 or nearly five times Ballard's original estimate, and the concern was deeply in debt.

Following the anticlimax of the opening, trade barely increased at all, and receipts were insufficient even to meet mortgage interest repayments. Efforts to cut losses by schemes for converting to a railway therefore continued unabated, but there were objections to the idea, not least a circuituous route and a long tunnel at Oxenhall that was too small for the purpose.

Nevertheless, just before completion to Hereford, overtures to the Welsh Midland Railway met with a promising response. Though the asking price was £150,000, an offer of £130,000 was deemed acceptable, but in the event the embryo company neither paid a deposit nor obtained its Act. Still intent on capitalising on the new vogue in transport, Ballard then wrote offering the canal to George Hudson the 'Railway King', but without avail.

In the autumn of 1845 a line was proposed from Gloucester to South Wales via Hereford on the course of the canal, with in addition a branch to Worcester from Ledbury. This project also came to nothing, and after the inevitable collapse of the Railway Mania the company had no alternative but to face reality and concentrate upon bolstering trade as best it could.

The realisation that Hereford would not after all achieve rail communication in the near future (it was in fact one of the last major towns in England to do so) brought a belated return of confidence, and by 1847 traffic sufficed to cover mortgage and loan interest charges. The growth of trade over the 20 years since thoughts first turned to the extension is indicated below.

	Gross Tonnage	Revenue
1828	6,410	£640 19s. 8d.
1838	16,030	£1,603 10s. 5d.
1848	43,080	£5,166 14s. 3d.

Business slowly continued to improve, and it became necessary to issue regulations concerning Oxenhall tunnel which had been built to a bore of about 9 ft only. To minimise the effect of this troublesome bottleneck the direction of boats was specified according to the time of day, those towards Gloucester being allowed through from 9 am-12 noon, 3 pm-12 pm and 3 am- 6 am. How different to the leisurely days of 20 years before, when nothing was permitted to move between sunset and sunrise! However, it appears that this sensible aid to traffic management was soon allowed to lapse, as we shall see in Chapter Seven.

Construction of the Shrewsbury-Hereford railway brought a transient gain in revenue, 130 tons of rails delivered to Widemarsh in September 1851 being an example of the traffic carried. The line opened in December 1853, to be followed a month later by the Newport, Abergavenny & Hereford Railway, and in June

EDWARD GEORGE,
TIMBER & SLATE
MERCHANT,
CANAL WHARF, HEREFORD,
NEW STREET, LEOMINSTER, & WITHINGTON,

HAS CONSTANTLY ON SALE

PRINCESS SLATES, 24in. by 14in.	FIRE BRICKS.
DUCHESS DITTO, 24in. by 12in.	FIRE BURS.
COUNTESS DITTO, 20in. by 10in.	OVEN SQUARES.
LADIES' DITTO, 16in. by 8in.	OATS.
RIDGE CRESS, Plain & Ornamental	LINSEED.
BROSELEY TILES, Ditto, Ditto	LINSEED CAKE.
FLOORING SQUARES, 8 & 9in.	COALS, &c., &c.

AGRICULTURAL, FINE, & ROCK SALT.

RICHARD SMITH, Etnam Street, Agent for Leominster ;
WILLIAM BIRD, Canal Wharf, Agent for Withington.

WILLIAM BIRD,
TIMBER & COAL MERCHANT,
Commission Agent,
AND
GENERAL WHARFINGER,
BROMYARD AND LEOMINSTER WHARFS,
WITHINGTON.

N.B.—Goods forwarded to all parts of the Kingdom.

Advertisements from Lascelles' Herefordshire Directory of 1851.

1855 by the Great Western broad gauge Gloucester-Hereford line via Ross. But notwithstanding direct rail access to the great manufacturing centres as well as the coalfields of Shropshire and Wales, traffic further increased to 47,560 tons in 1858. Methods adopted included rate-cutting incentives, and an agreement with the Newport, Abergavenny & Hereford whereby Monmouthshire coal could be conveyed cheaply by water as far as Newent - incidentally leading to the spectacle of coal from different regions travelling in opposing directions over the same canal.

Some idea of the commercial activity at this time could be gleaned from Casset's *Directory of Herefordshire* which listed these companies having representatives at the city basin.

Mouseley & Co. - Boats to all parts of the Kingdom
Pickford & Co. (J. Holloway, agent) - London and all parts
Danks, Venn & Saunders (Joseph Fawke, agent) - London and all parts
Mounsell & Co. (Reuben Kernish, agent) - London and all parts
Robert Smallwood - Birmingham

Danks, Venn & Saunders boats left Gloucester daily for Hereford 'from which latter place goods are conveyed expeditiously by railway to Leominster, Kington, Ludlow etc. and by wagons, daily to Weobley, Builth, Hay, Glasbury, Talgarth etc'.

The year 1860 was to represent a high water mark with tolls amounting to £7,061, but as in the instance of the Thames & Severn Canal, such ostensibly favourable results reflected an ominous development creating a temporary traffic in materials of construction. This was the Worcester & Hereford Railway, a line which had for long been projected, and one for which the canal company had willingly withheld objections in exchange for a railway conversion deal. The tumultuous origins of the Worcester & Hereford were well recorded by E.T. MacDermot and we cannot do better than to quote his words:

Two rival schemes for a railway between the Cities of Worcester and Hereford were projected in 1846; one, part of the Welsh Midland Railway, backed by the Midland Company, the other, a broad-gauge line laid out under Brunel's auspices, to connect the Oxford, Worcester & Wolverhampton with the [proposed] Monmouth & Hereford Railway. Both were abandoned in the following year and nothing more was done till 1851, when Captain Huish and the London & North Western Directors took the matter up as a first step in their invasion of South Wales, to connect their ally, the Midland, with the Newport, Abergavenny & Hereford, which they had every hope of annexing.

A line was accordingly laid out by Charles Liddell from the south end of the Shrub Hill Station of the Oxford, Worcester & Wolverhampton Railway to cross the Severn and the Teme south of the City and, leaving Malvern Link well on the left, proceed by Cradley and Bosbury to the Herefordshire & Gloucestershire Canal, part of which was to be used for the railway, and so on to . . . the City of Hereford. Both Malvern and Ledbury were thus left to be served by branches to the no small discontent of those towns. A Bill for this line was promoted in the session of 1852 ostensibly by an independent company, but really by the London & North Western, Midland, and Newport, Abergavenny & Hereford. After a long and strenuous fight it passed the Commons, only to be rejected by the Lords, upon which the promotors announced their intention of trying again next year.

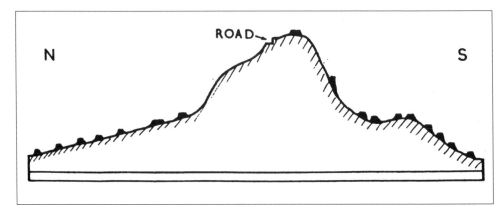

A section along Oxenhall tunnel, showing the 17 shaft-mounds still surviving in 1836. The vertical scale is exaggerated. According to the Ordnance Survey, the shafts were not even in line when sunk.

Directly above Oxenhall tunnel in 1976, looking south towards the entrance at the fourth hedge. The pump raised water from the tunnel after closure, and the bushy mound marks a shaft; both have now gone.   *Author*

Preparations were accordingly made by both sides for a decisive battle in 1853. The Great Western joined with the Oxford, Worcester & Wolverhampton, whom they were fighting bitterly on everything else, to promote the Worcester & Hereford Junction Railway, in opposition to the Worcester & Hereford Railway of the North Western, Midland, and Newport, Abergavenny & Hereford Companies.

After a stiff fight in the Commons the Worcester & Hereford promoters won the day, although not without drastic revision to Liddell's route. In particular both Great Malvern and Ledbury were to be served directly, the line then striking straight across country to its destination avoiding the canal altogether. Thus, in spite of the prior understanding, the canal company now faced the worst of both worlds, its proprietors' concept of a waterway convertible from Ledbury to Hereford having proved worthless at last.

A disused underpass in the Prior's Court embankment across the Leadon Valley, built large enough for hay wagons.   *Author*

W.P. Price, 1817-1891.   *The late Peter Price*

Chapter Six

Under Railway Control

Subsequent to 1845 the destiny of the Hereford & Gloucester Canal was in great measure influenced by William Philip Price of Tibberton Court. The son of William Price (1788-1838) of Gloucester, he was born in 1817 and entered the family timber business. He soon revealed talents in public and commercial matters, becoming a member of the canal committee and a JP in his mid-twenties, and Sheriff of Gloucester a few years later. When only 22 he was a founder of the Gloucestershire Chamber of Commerce, and represented the city as MP for the greater part of the years 1852-73.

But it was in the world of transport that Price excelled. He was for instance in 1870 Chairman of the Midland and Gloucester & Dean Forest Railways, the Gloucester & Berkeley Canal, the Hereford & Gloucester Canal, and one of the Severn Commissioners. Richard Potter his partner in business was no less distinguished, being at different times Chairman of the Great Western Railway, President of the Grand Trunk Railway of Canada and virtual owner of the Thames & Severn Canal.

With so many allegiances Price rather resembled W.S. Gilbert's *Pooh-Bah* and we are bound to marvel how the inevitable conflicts were reconciled. A keen sense of humour was another of his attributes and many were the Board meetings enlivened by his presence. Price's affairs prospered, leading to an appointment as Railway Commissioner in 1873 at a salary of £3,000 per year, a position which he retained until his death in 1891.

Although born with a silver spoon in his mouth (his father gave him Tibberton Court as a combined 21st birthday and wedding present), Price was always mindful of those in less fortunate circumstances. Over 20 years before education became compulsory, he built the village school, paid for its teacher, and insisted it was 'to be entirely undenominational in regard to the religious instruction afforded'. As a Unitarian he had been denied access to University and gained his Doctorate of Literature at a private institution.

He improved the drainage of large areas of land, opened a reading room for the village, built large new houses for his workmen, and endowed four almshouses 'for aged or infirm persons who would otherwise be probably compelled to end their days in the Union Workhouse'.

Against such a backcloth W.P. Price's long and intimate role in the management of the Hereford & Gloucester Canal has to be viewed. In his eyes it could hardly have amounted to much, yet he served its interests well. Perhaps it was a question of old loyalties, for many years previously in appreciation of services rendered, its proprietors had presented his grandfather with a splendid service of plate - a testimonial that remains in the family to this day.

Among the contractors for the Worcester & Hereford Railway was a partnership of two men, one of whom was Thomas Brassey. The other was Stephen Ballard, who had been taken under the latter's wing whilst working in the Fens. Ballard's standing had risen by this time and the new line was actually to pass through an

The very narrow lock on the Severn at Maisemore, built for traffic on the Hereford & Gloucester Canal.   *Author*

estate which he had meanwhile acquired at Colwall. Whilst the line was under construction, further development arose which culminated in the amalgamation on 1st July, 1860 of three railway companies - the Oxford, Worcester & Wolverhampton, the Newport, Abergavenny & Hereford (of which W.P. Price was Chairman) and the Worcester & Hereford under the joint title of the West Midland Railway. Of particular significance was that among those serving upon the new Board were W.P. Price as deputy Chairman, and his partner Richard Potter.

Price at this time held a powerful position in railway and canal circles within the three counties, and the fate of the Hereford & Gloucester Canal, of which he was also Chairman, lay virtually in the palm of his hand. After the Worcester-Hereford line via Ledbury opened in 1861 he took the only possible course, and approached the Chairman of the Great Western Railway. 'I appealed to Lord Shelburne', he recorded, 'and asked the Great Western Company to take the canal off our hands . . . my fear would be that if this was not carried out the canal must of necessity be closed and without getting a railway we should lose the only mode of communication which we have'. This was certainly true, with Price himself together with his tenants at Tibberton personally concerned about the consequences.

The upshot of the meeting was an agreement concluded with the Great Western and the West Midland companies on 17th January, 1862. It contained a proviso to permit conversion of the canal to a railway from Ledbury to Gloucester, which Price afterwards claimed had been inserted solely at the request of the West Midland.

In further detail, the agreement provided for management of the canal by a joint committee representing the three companies until an Act of Parliament was obtained to ratify the transfer of ownership, after which an annual rental of £5,000 would be payable in perpetuity. And until such time as an Act might be passed, the canal company would receive 90 per cent of gross receipts independent of working expenses.

The politics behind this important development were no doubt more subtle than Price pretended, for the new owners would hardly have taken over an obsolescent navigation in the midst of their own territory as an act of charity; perhaps the spectre of a rival railway such as the Midland making a bid provided the spur. The concept of a lease instead of outright purchase was also unusual in such circumstances. As for the West Midland, its influence was transient; it became absorbed by the Great Western empire on 1st August, 1863, and henceforth after 70 chequered years the Hereford & Gloucester Canal became virtually a puppet of the latter company alone.

On the whole, Price had made a good bargain, although the full annual income of £5,000 was not to materialize for a number of years. The reasons were these: the Great Western having gained control, was in no hurry to sanctify the agreement with the promised Act, and had little real intent of implementing the conversion clause. There was also a further cause for delay, occasioned by the ephemeral Worcester, Dean Forest & Monmouth Railway which was intended to run via Newent and Mitcheldean. Its Act was obtained on 21st July, 1863 and a further Act authorised a branch from Newent to Gloucester. This of course presented another possibility of conversion, upon which negotiations took place between the Great Western and the Dean Forest companies.

In the event the project collapsed in the financial crisis which depressed railway stock during the mid-1860s, but not before half a mile of heavy earthworks had been completed for a tunnel approach north-east of Newent. The earthworks are still to be found between Pauntley Church and Brand Green. (For further details of this project see H.W. Paar *The Great Western Railway in Dean*, 1965.) By this time the Great Western had no incentive other than a moral one to satisfy the 1862 agreement, especially since the annual payment would substantially increase thereby, and only after persistent lobbying did it take the plunge in 1870.

Objections immediately arose from the Severn Commissioners, the Staffordshire & Worcestershire Canal, and carriers who feared the worst from railway domination. In defence, the Great Western strongly denied any plans for conversion, and stressed that it had actually a double interest in keeping the canal open because of its revenue earning capacity, and because under the Oxford, Worcester & Wolverhampton Railway Act of 1845 it was obliged to make up to the Severn Commissioners any deficiency in river tolls falling below an aggregate of £14,000 per annum. The current deficit amounted to about £6,000, and there seems little doubt that the protestations were genuine.

Nevertheless the objectors remained suspicious, John Owen Saunders of Danks, Venn & Saunders asserting that maintenance had suffered under the joint management. His firm contributed by far the largest traffic on the canal, more than one-third of the whole. Rates had not been altered, but certain rebates allowed by the old company had been rescinded. Other objectors were the Staffordshire & Worcestershire Canal Company and the Severn Commissioners, but the Bill passed the Commons practically without amendment. The Great Western Railway (Hereford & Gloucester Canal Vesting) Act received the Royal Assent on 4th July, 1870.

Meanwhile, what of traffic on the canal since the Worcester & Hereford Railway opened in 1861? It had inevitably diminished, but by no means excessively, due to the good management and economy which the company had practised almost from the day of its foundation. The chief expedients were drastic rate-cutting, particularly for coal going the full 34 miles to Hereford, for which Danks, Venn & Saunders paid only 1s. per ton for the whole distance, or about ⅓d. per mile. In the words of W.P. Price: 'That rate was made for the express purpose of leaving the Staffordshire and Worcestershire coal owners the only opportunity we could give them of maintaining their connection with Hereford'.

Saunders himself claimed that any increase would destroy the traffic altogether and we have only to glance at the map to see the reason. 'Whenever we could show that we could introduce a large quantity on the canal', Saunders continued, 'they have taken a liberal view and made concessions time after time'. A similar circumstance applied to foreign timber where the rate was 2s. 6d., upon which a drawback or rebate of 1s. was allowed, at least until the joint committee took over.

Thus was tonnage maintained, but not without a heavy fall in revenue. The loss of Hereford traffic was not, however, of great significance, for like the trade mission of old, the canal's business lay most of all in what it accomplished on the way.

After 1861 coal to Newent and various wharves constituted much of the revenue. There was also limestone from Ledbury and building stone from

Clifford's Mesne as well as slate, timber, salt, groceries and sundry other merchandize. Bricks came up from brickyards alongside the Severn and there was a substantial traffic in grain and cider. Reductions in rates were also granted to R.F. Onslow for iron-ore from his mines near Newent, not that the output ever amounted to much. Richard Francis Onslow died in 1849, he was archdeacon of Worcester and 47 years vicar of Newent. His son, Richard Foley Onslow, resided at Stardens, Newent, and was Lord of the Manor until his death in 1879.

An idea of the canal's income and expenses during its long decline is given by the following table for the half-year ending 31st December, 1862.

Income	£	s	d	Expenses	£	s	d
Tonnages	1,721	13	2	Wages	502	19	0
Weighing	46	10	1	Salaries	150	0	0
Rents	106	1	0	Repairs	104	0	4
	1,874	4	3	Rates, Taxes	64	5	9
				Incidentals	70	5	9
Balance	982	13	5		891	10	10

Revenue for the full year fell to £2,384 10s. 9d. for 1868, with a tonnage of 28,080. By comparing this with figures for 20 years previously we can see that rate-cutting had limited the fall in tonnage to 35 per cent, but at a cost penalty of 54 per cent. However, because of the 90 per cent revenue agreement the canal company actually did very well, receiving some £10,000 more over the period 1862-69 than if it had remained independent.

The general pattern of trade from 1870 onwards was reflected by the tonnage entering the canal from the Severn, mostly from the down-river direction;

Year	Tonnage	Year	Tonnage
1870	8,031	1876	5,970
1871	7,228	1877	4,921
1872	-	1878	4,805
1873	5,825	1879	-
1874	4,167	1880	4,328
1875	5,575	1881	4,895

An interesting development on the Severn to accommodate river-borne traffic destined for the Hereford & Gloucester Canal in its later years, was the construction of Maisemore lock, a mile upstream from Over. How this came about is related by Charles Hadfield in his *Canals of the West Midlands*.

The Severn Commissioners had long been troubled by low water on the eastern side of Alney Island impeding navigation, and to remedy this, by an Act of 1869, they built a weir on the western branch above Maisemore. It was completed in 1870, together with a narrow-boat lock in the following year. This lock was in fact, extremely tight, being only 7 ft 3 in. wide and 73 ft long. Coal barges continued to use it bound for Maisemore wharf for some time after the canal closed, and it still remains in a reasonably good state, though badly silted up.

Eighteen-eighty constituted the last complete year of normal business, for the GWR published notification of closure between Ledbury and the Severn from

HEREFORD AND GLOUCESTER CANAL — Pay Bill for the Fortnight ending 30 July 1876

Name	Occupation	Locality	Time (Days)	Weekly Rate s	Weekly Rate d	Wages £	Wages s	Wages d	Rent Deductions £	Rent Deductions s	Rent Deductions d	Amount to Receive £	Amount to Receive s	Amount to Receive d
Baylis, M.	Lock keeper & Ticket Clerk	Over Lock	14	21	—	2	2	—		6	—	1	16	—
Freeman, William	Lock keeper	Rudford	14	14	—	1	8	—		4	—	1	4	—
Winters, John	Lock keeper	Coneybury	14	13	—	1	6	—		2	—	1	4	—
Stinge, John	Lock keeper	Bullocks Lock	14	13	—	1	6	—		2	—	1	4	—
Preece, John	Lock keeper	Oxenhall	14	14	—	1	8	—		4	—	1	4	—
Bayley, Richard	Lock keeper	Leathermill	14	14	—	1	8	—		4	—	1	4	—
Davis, Edmund	Lock keeper	Ledbury	14	14	—	1	8	—		4	—	1	4	—
Jones, Richard	Lock keeper	Bars Lock	14	13	6	1	7	—		3	—	1	4	—
Thomas, George	Lock keeper	Withington	14	2	6		5	—		4	—		1	—
Morton, John	Water Bailiff	Ashperton	14	14	—	1	8	—		4	—	1	4	—
Bowkett, Sydney	Wharfinger	Newent	14	20	—	2	2	—		4	—	1	16	—
Paytherm, Richard	Wharfinger	Ledbury	14	21	—	2	2	—		6	—	1	16	—
Napper, John	Inspector	Withington	14	35	—	3	10	—		4	—	3	6	—
Goode, George	Labourer	Hereford	14	16	6	1	13	—		4	—	1	9	—
Napper, William	Carpenter	Ledbury	12	3	9*	2	5	—		—		2	5	—
Napper, Jabes	Carpenter	Ledbury	12	2	6*	1	10	—		—		1	10	—
Thomas, George	Labourer	Withington	12	2	8*	1	12	—		—		1	12	—
Hill, Henry	Labourer	Withington	12	2	8*	1	12	—		—		1	12	—
Tylor, William	Labourer	Withington	10	2	8*	1	6	8		—		1	6	8
Godsall, Thomas	Labourer	Withington	2	2	8*		5	4		—			5	4
						31	2	—	2	15	—	28	7	—
Maddox, Thomas	Wharfinger	Hereford	28	21	6	4	6	—		14	—	3	12	—
Maddox, Thomas	Book keeper	Hereford	28	£80 +		6	2	9		—		6	2	9
Ballard, Philip	Manager	Hereford	28	£200 +		15	6	10		—		15	6	10
						56	17	7	3	9	—	53	8	7

*Per day   + Per annum

Reproduced by courtesy of C.F. Ballard, Esq.

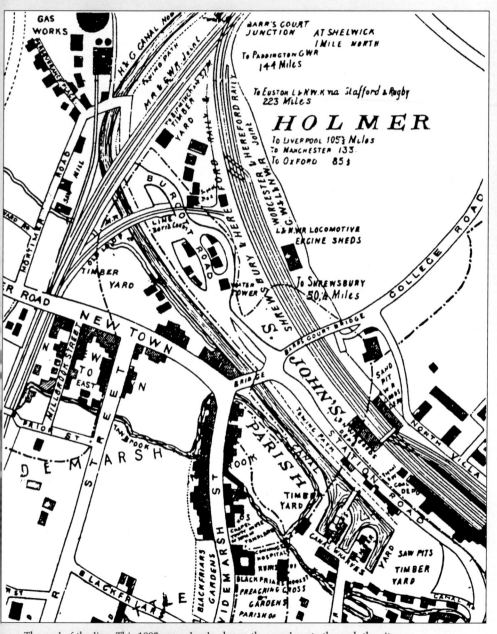

The end of the line. This 1885 map clearly shows the canal route through the city.

Hereford Library

30th June, 1881 to permit construction of the Ledbury-Gloucester Railway, as described later. Although the length of canal still functioning gradually diminished as the new line advanced eastwards, contractors' traffic contributed to an actual rise over the previous year. But in 1882 tonnage fell to 2,853, and to 348 in 1883. The very last figures were for the week ending 18th August for a cargo of 19 tons bound for Diglis, near Worcester.

Thus the Hereford & Gloucester Canal died. It was a sad conclusion but swift and honourable, and better than the rotting dereliction that signified the last decades of many another inland navigation. Several years after the canal had closed, Philip Ballard, who had been its manager ever since 1845, was murdered in his home at Tupsley. The outrage created a sensation, and two men hung for the crime were modelled in wax at Madame Tussauds.

As for the fate of the canal after abandonment, those parts which were not destroyed by the Gloucester-Ledbury railway were gradually sold off under an Act of 1882. However, as late as 1906, Herefordshire County Council was expressing regret that the Hereford-Ledbury section had not been kept open for the benefit of riparian landowners and communities which it passed through; it is more than possible that stretches here and there unofficially served such a purpose, at least for a year or two.

Much of the route was hardly saleable at any price. A dwelling often served to sugar the pill, as in 1889 at Canon Frome, where the wharf-house and outbuildings went to John Hopton for £375. But the purchase encumbered him with two miles of canal that nobody wanted, stretching from the Yarkhill road through Ashperton tunnel to Moorend Farm, some 24 acres that had doubtless cost the company dear, half a century before.

But though the waterway had gone, the days of the company were not yet over. It carried on for a further 65 years, distributing the £5,000 annual income until nationalization finally closed the books in 1948. Preference shares had risen from £20 to £30 immediately following the 1870 Act, and thereafter dividends of 7½ per cent were paid. In most years preference shareholders also received an additional 1 per cent as a contribution towards wiping out arrears that had accumulated, and they eventually became entitled to an equivalent value of British Transport Stock at an arbitrated valuation.

Based on such evidence we may truly observe that the canal's best years came when it ceased to convey any traffic at all. And in this unexpected way, those false hopes and disappointments met some compensation at last.

HEREFORDSHIRE AND GLOUCESTERSHIRE CANAL.

In the Matter of the Newent Railway Act, 1873, and in the Matter of the Ross and Ledbury Railway Act, 1873.

TAKE NOTICE, that in pursuance of the powers in that behalf contained in the Newent Railway Act, 1873, and the Ross and Ledbury Railway Act, 1873, it is intended on and after the 30th day of June, 1881, TO STOP UP AND CLOSE so much and such part of the CANAL known as the Herefordshire and Gloucestershire Canal as is situate BETWEEN the Worcester and Hereford Railway at LEDBURY, in the county of Hereford, and the River Severn, in the City of GLOUCESTER, and that all rights of way or navigation, and other rights and privileges, if any, along, upon, or over such part of the said Canal, with the banks and towing path, will as from the said 30th day of June, cease and determine accordingly.

AND FURTHER TAKE NOTICE, that all persons who will be affected by the closing of the said portion of the Canal are required, on or before the said 30th day of June, to remove their Barges, Boats, and other Craft accordingly.

Dated this 2nd day of June, 1881.
6140   By Order.

Chapter Seven

The Daily Round

Even the relative tranquility of inland waterways sometimes brought home to boatmen the dangers of the mariner, and especially was this so upon the tidal reaches of the Severn near Over lock, where a number of bad accidents occurred. Typical examples were on 2nd November, 1867 when two boats belonging to John Hodgetts of Staplow Wharf sunk on entering the river, and on Christmas Day 1869, when a boat of Samuel Hodgetts of Newent was driven hard against the abutments of Maisemore bridge and smashed to pieces. The lock gates at Over also took a heavy pounding. One broke up and disappeared in the Severn in November 1841 but was replaced within a few days. Another incident took place on 31st March, 1835 involving one of the canal company's boats and hazardous remnants of the ancient bridge which Telford's splendid arch of a single span had only recently superseded. According to Ballard's diaries:

Instead of passing between the piers of the old Over bridge (this was the medieval bridge, downstream of Telford's bridge) [recorded Stephen Ballard], she struck against one of them and her stern swung round across two of the other piers that were taken down just low enough for the boat to go on them - and as the tide was running strong against the side of the boat the men on board could not get her off, but the stern was heaved off with a lever - into the deep hole below the bridge - this done with an idea that it would prevent her upsetting. She was loaded with coal and slate about 27 tons. As soon as I heard of the accident I had an empty boat taken from the quay (at Gloucester) and all the coal and slate that was above water taken out of the boat. Then borrowed a Balk and a large spar and a pit roll (windlass) of Mr Armstrong, who very kindly offered assistance, the person who was taking down the old bridge. The spar and balk placed on one of the piers of the old bridge and the other ends on the boat that was brought from the quay with a chain fastened round the sunken boat - and passing round the pit roll wound her up so that the water could be baled out which was done in a few minutes and the remainder of the lading was soon transferred when we were enabled to launch the boat off the piers into the water and found she had sustained scarcely any damage. Had she remained in the state I found her till the new tide most likely the whole of the cargo would have been lost and the boat would have been much damaged and a much greater expense incurred in rising her - it was dark before she was got off the piers.

Locks were another danger. In 1831, only one all the way to Ledbury had a hand-rail on the gates, so that crossing over was tantamount to walking a plank 9 inches wide. Such was the hazard in darkness and bad weather, that in recent years a lock-keeper and a poor woman had met their deaths, apart from many narrow escapes.

Oxenhall tunnel, with a narrow and crooked bore lacking a single passing-place in its entire 1¼ miles, was always dreaded, not least for the risk of meeting another boat. Although traffic control was introduced in 1849, it could not have lasted long, as we can gather from the following incident, which for its duration must rank unique in the annals of British canals.

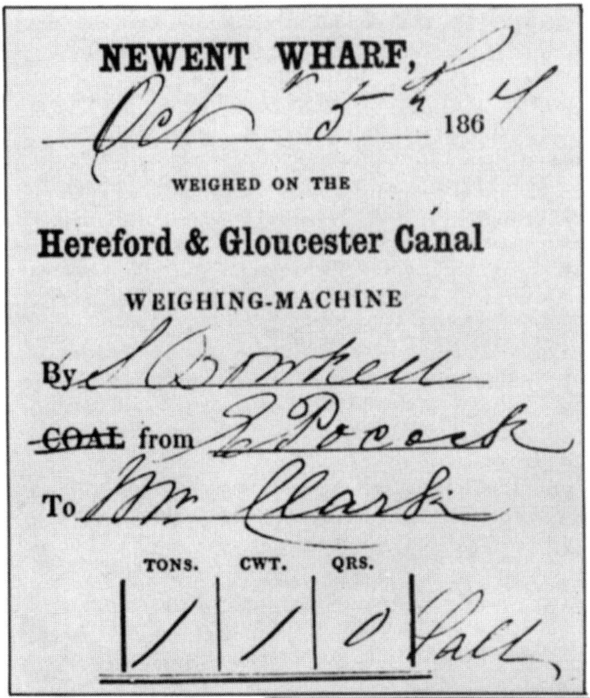

NEWENT WHARF,

Oct 5th 186*4*

WEIGHED ON THE

Hereford & Gloucester Canal

WEIGHING-MACHINE

By *(signature)*

~~COAL~~ from *(signature)*

To *(signature)*

TONS.	CWT.	QRS.
1	1	0

The old order changeth. Weighbridge tickets before and after the GWR took control.

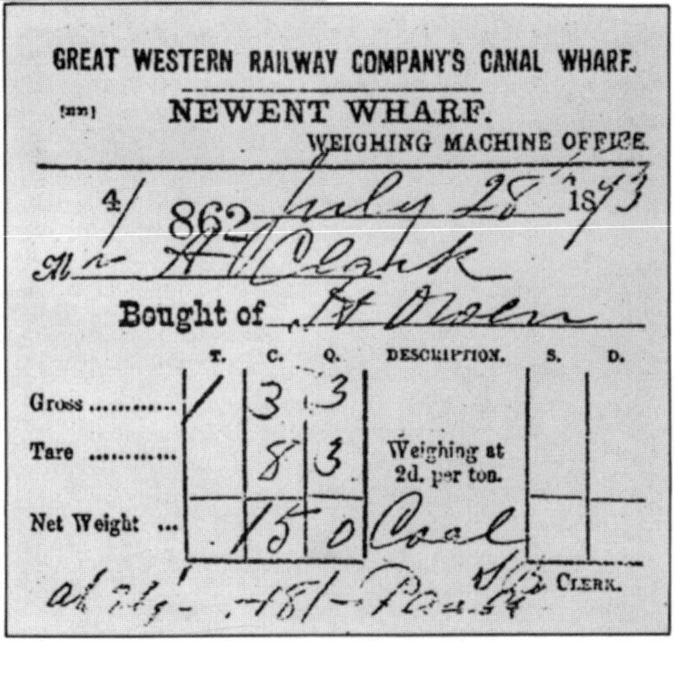

GREAT WESTERN RAILWAY COMPANY'S CANAL WHARF.

NEWENT WHARF.

WEIGHING MACHINE OFFICE.

4/862 *July 28 1873*

Mr H Clark

Bought of *(signature)*

	T.	C.	Q.	DESCRIPTION.	S.	D.
Gross	1	3	3			
Tare		8	3	Weighing at 2d. per ton.		
Net Weight		15	0	Coal		

(signature) CLERK.

In May 1851, the *Hereford Times* reported a charge of impeding the navigation brought before the Newent bench by Philip Ballard. About midnight one Thursday, a barge belonging to a Mr Collingbourne of Gloucester had entered the tunnel and met another mid-way through, owned by a Mr Smith of the Kerry Arms, Hereford. Each refused to retreat, and more barges soon crowded behind, all in total darkness, except perhaps for an oil lamp or two.

What ensued, entombed in that dripping and subterranean prison with no means of relief or escape, can only be left to the imagination. Incredible though it seems, the tunnel was not cleared until 10 am *on the following Sunday,* by which time no doubt one or other of the protagonists had collapsed through sheer exhaustion.

According to the local press, another serious incident occurred in July 1853 when an exceptional cloudburst over Dymock caught a number of boats going northwards through the tunnel. Mr Goode, the lock-keeper at Oxenhall, where no rain had fallen, was astonished to see a flow of water down the canal such that it eventually rose to the third step in his cottage, but then rapidly receded due to the bursting of the banks near Dymock. The plight of the boatmen deep underground must have been fearful, with the water rising so high as practically to crush the vessels against the roof.

Impediments to navigation also arose since, in spite of the promoters' assurances, in dry seasons the water supply to the summit level never really sufficed for the purpose. As an instance, 18 laden boats grounded near Canon Frome in August 1864, and in October 1872 only very light loads could be carried. The long stretch below Rudford lock was also very vulnerable due to the heavy thirst of the deep lock into the Severn.

Winters during the19th century were generally worse than at present, and interruption of traffic due to frost recurred frequently. We shall see later how Ballard invented an improved ice-breaking boat, but sometimes nothing could be done. Early in 1871 the canal froze for several weeks, and six horses had a heavy job hauling an ice-boat the whole distance from Hereford to the Severn.

The potential power of water as an agent of destruction was illustrated on 5th April, 1830 by a spectacular failure of the main arch of Leathermill aqueduct. About five square feet of masonry blew out into the Leadon, and 20 cubic yards of clay-puddle lining were washed away by the torrent. Twenty men 'with great exertion' managed to form a temporary seal with planks, and the channel was full again by 10 pm the same day.

The boats trading upon the canal call for no particular mention, being common to those generally found on narrow canals, but an observation of Stephen Ballard's on 1st December, 1838 is worth recording. 'Saw the Eastnor Castle in Newent Wharf under repair. She has only been built 9 or 10 years but being foreign oak, where there is no air the timber is rotten.'

Maintenance was a constant drain on revenue. By 1818, the whole line needed dredging, and in 1831, six pairs of lock-gates were described as 'entirely worn out'. Four years later the question of a new wooden draw-bridge at Newent had to be faced. Ballard replaced it with a fixed cast-iron structure raised three feet higher to clear the boats, at a cost of some £128. However, swing and draw-bridges survived for many years, in some places until the very end. The first edition Ordnance maps show no less than seven between Over and Newent.

This simple milestone reflected the poverty of the company. Two more, 21½ and 22, have been removed to a private site.   *Author*

Oxenhall tunnel with nowhere to pass, and here excavated in solid New Red Sandstone. Silting at the ends had raised the water four or five feet.   *Alan Simpson*

Repairs were largely confined to summer months when traffic was lighter. Some idea of financial inflation since those days can be gathered from the bill for painting the outside of 11 of the company's houses in 1863; the charge inclusive of labour came to £18 14s. 0d. or £1 14s. 0d. per house.

Inland waterways for pleasure were becoming popular by the 1870s, when a party of young men canoed along the canal to Hereford and then down the River Wye. Their experiences formed the basis of one, if not two, accounts published independently some years ago, in which the weedy state of the channel and general lack of traffic was noted.

A journey of a valedictory nature was made by canoe in the last year or two of the canal's life by Alfred Watkins, a well known photographer who was to become famous as author of *The Old Straight Track*. His purpose was to record the route, but unfortunately only one or two pictures seem to survive.

Another observer of the canal in its last days was John Masefield, to whom as a child living nearby at Ledbury it was a source of wonder and delight. His recollections were vivid.

> . . . the woman steering with her most becoming head-dress of a milkmaid's cap flapping on her cheeks, and the husband ahead minding the horse, and often singing, or knitting, or flinging words over his shoulder to the wife.
> Sometimes these glorious people begged the little boy to come aboard, and showed me the marvellous cabin, bright as a new pin, with its bunks and gear, the most wonderful abodes on earth. I was not often in Bye Street [he continued] but believed that it was their Sailor Town, and that there when lamps were lit and little boys in bed, they would make merry, and tell of the dangers of the deep.

Perhaps those days were the inspiration that made Masefield the seaman's poet; at all events we can well believe that his long romance with boats and water began on the banks of the Hereford & Gloucester Canal.

A cast-iron column for supporting a crane at Ashperton wharf, 1977. *Author*

Right: Commemorating the unveiling of a plaque on the restoration of Tunnel House, Ashperton, June 1986. *Left to right;* the author, Stephen Ballard the engineer's grandson, and Michael Peach the owner. *Mike Potts*

Below: Fruits of restoration. Major Barnes' boat *Brindley* at the Skew Bridge, Monkhide, during an Open Weekend, May 1992. *Mike Potts*

Chapter Eight

The Herefordshire and Gloucestershire Canal Trust

When, over 20 years ago, the first edition of this history suggested the possibility of opening up old towpaths and stretches of canal here and there, it was never supposed that within a decade, a full-blown Trust would aim towards resurrecting all 34 miles from end to end. How, from faltering beginnings this came about, and what has been accomplished, may briefly be told as follows.

Late in 1979, I put forward a proposal to restore 400 yards of canal near Newent lake, concerning which two articles appeared in waterways publications. A feasibility study was submitted to Newent Town Council and work actually began, but was eventually abandoned following a report by the Inland Waterways Protection Society drawing attention to potential problems.

Currently, there were also suggestions for a society to preserve remaining sections of the canal and buildings, but the time was not ripe. However, these attempts sowed some seeds, and in July 1980, under the heading Canal Potential, a long letter appeared in the *Hereford Times*, but not until the autumn of 1982 was a Steering Committee formed. This led to the inaugural meeting of the Herefordshire & Gloucestershire Canal Society on 13th April, 1983 at the Red Cross Hall, Hereford, a circumstance not without a certain irony bearing in mind the city's cool reception to the canal in its formative years. But this time there was more enthusiasm; the first field meeting was a well attended trip to the Withington area, and very popular it proved.

In the beginning, the aims of the society were modest enough, the idea of limited restoration being listed merely as something to be explored. But the idea proved increasingly alluring, not least, due to the kind consent granted by Major Robert Barnes, a descendant of Stephen Ballard, to clear a section of canal on land at Monkhide. A notable landmark was the erection of a plaque on the remarkable skew bridge, bearing the words 'Hereford & Gloucester Canal. Skew Bridge 1843. HGCS 1985.', the first of a number along the route. The society also gained a Grade II Listing for the structure.

The summer of 1987 saw a length of canal re-opened at Monkhide on the second Open Day amid celebrations, and a small steam-boat was launched in the following year.

Demands now intensified for a far more ambitious objective, no less than total restoration of the whole route, even though many bridges and nearly all the 21 locks had gone without trace, not to mention miles of route returned to agriculture. The vision soon became official policy.

In the summer of 1990 a display at the National Waterways Festival, Gloucester, attracted many new members from all over the country. The next year the Society had a battle on its hands regarding the proposed A49/A465 Hereford Bypass which threatened to block the line of the canal to the north-east of the city. By good fortune the Chairman, Cliff Penny, happened to be a

Early stages of restoration at Over Basin. The corner of the wharf from the rear.
Penny Environmental & Planning

Chartered Civil Engineer and his detailed evidence caused the Department of Transport to call for adjournments of the Public Inquiry. He proved the Department to be wrong on a number of counts, and their costs in relation to accommodating the canal to be over double what they should have been. The Inspectors' recommendation to the Secretaries of State for the Environment, and Transport, that the road contract should include a navigable culvert, was eventually accepted.

At Easter 1991, restoration of half a mile of canal from the southern portal of Oxenhall tunnel towards Newent commenced in earnest with the assistance of the Waterway Recovery Group. The great public interest in this tunnel may be gauged from the fact that three talks, illustrated with colour slides and a unique 8mm cine film taken underground at considerable risk some 30 years before, attracted over 500 people.

A significant development was the formation in 1992 of the Herefordshire and Gloucestershire Canal Trust and Trading Company as a vital step in obtaining more Grant Aid, and by 1994 the Trust had nearly 600 members from all over the country, including corporate membership from an impressive list of local and national businesses. It is now over a thousand.

After restoring nearly a mile of the route on each side of the A4103 road at Crew's Pitch in 1985, attention turned to the Newent area, where the owner had generously donated to the Trust the derelict Lock Cottage and lock together with a length of canal. The cottage was sold to a local farmer and has since been tastefully restored and occupied whilst conforming to Listed Building regulations. Volunteers have also made great progress in restoring the lock chamber and surrounding structures.

Probably the most impressive work thus far completed is at the start of the canal at Over where it leaves the River Severn. The area included a lock, wharf and basin, much of which was buried under vegetation and many feet of infill in the grounds of an abandoned hospital. By agreement with the developers of the site, sterling efforts by the Waterways Recovery Group and local volunteers enabled restoration of the wharf and basin, together with a length of canal, to be finished with a week to spare before a grand opening ceremony in September 2000. This will also provide a substantial amenity for the new estate now erected close by, and a derelict lock cottage has been demolished to make way for a new wharf house and reception centre.

Meanwhile, at Hereford, by agreement between the Trust, local authority and the developers, two new concrete bridges were built where a revised line of canal would pass through a new retail park. Further discussions are in hand to excavate the bed and adjoining sections which have long since been infilled. More details of the various restoration projects are given in Chapter Nine.

These latest initiatives were only achieved by the close collaboration initiated by the Herefordshire & Gloucestershire Canal Trust between all parties concerned. Finally, the Trust has asked me to record their appreciation for the support of the landowners both along the line of the canal, the Inland Waterways Association, Waterway Recovery Group, the various Councils and Grant Aid bodies, and all the volunteers who have devoted their time to these major works.

Over Basin slipway showing restoration of first section of canal, August 2000.

Penny Environmental & Planning

Over Basin in Summer 2000.   *Penny Environmental & Planning*

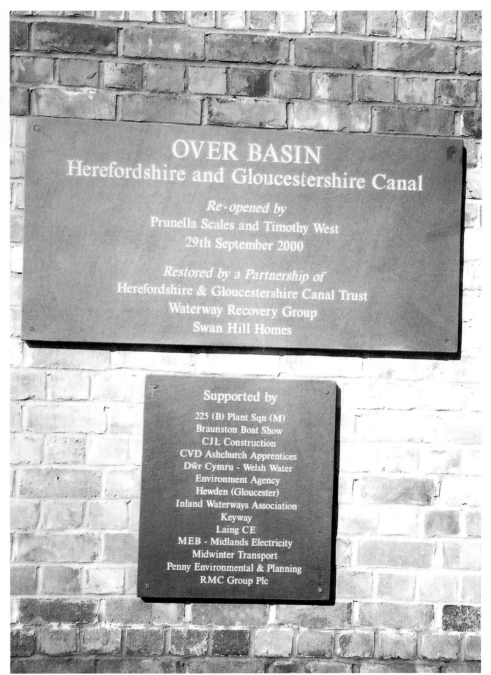

Over Basin, the official Phase I plaques.   *Penny Environmental & Planning*

The new road bridge over the future line of the canal at Hereford Retail Park.
Penny Environmental & Planning

A view from beneath the new road bridge at Hereford Retail Park showing the new footbridge.
Penny Environmental & Planning

At the time of writing, proposals for future developments have yet to be announced. Further details of the Trust and its activities, together with lecture programmes, visits etc., can be obtained from:

The Membership Secretary,
H&G Canal Trust,
6, Castle Street,
Hereford,
HR1 2NL

The Trust website is www.h-g-canal.org.uk

The restored Lock Cottage in 1998.

Then and now. Alfred Watkins' photograph of the lock at Rudford *c.*1882, and the scene as it is today. The man is standing on the site of the cottage.   *Hereford Public Library and Author*

Chapter Nine

Along the Towpath

'. . . there was the feeling that all that path by all that clear water must lead to Paradise.'
John Masefield

As we have seen, the canal on either side of Ledbury belonged to different centuries, and this is clearly apparent when we come to follow the route on the ground, or to study its course on old maps.

The earlier section reveals every trait of a Brindley canal, pursuing a leisurely course astride contours almost as a river meanders, with little attempt to shorten distance by cuttings or embankments - a contrast to Ballard's route which conforms more to the bolder Telford tradition, although admittedly losing some charm in the process. The rather serpentine mile west of Ashperton tunnel forms no exception, for it was also a product of the 18th century. These early and late characteristics of the canal era will manifest themselves constantly as we explore. We shall also observe that in addition to an undisturbed length of three miles at Oxenhall, relics of the line to Ledbury survive in the manner of a sine-wave crossing and re-crossing the usurping railway.

Originally, the canal crossed Alney Island from below Westgate bridge, Gloucester, but this short length was soon abandoned due to silting, and nothing shows of it now.

Thereafter the canal effectively began from the west bank of the Severn directly opposite the Alney cut, where a deep lock raised its level sufficient to pass over an aqueduct below which ran the River Leadon, acting as a millrace for Over Cornmill. The site of the latter is now beneath the approach road to the new bridge. The junction with the river is now indistinguishable, though the chamber still survives although largely buried. This was the only lock spared by construction of the railway as far as Newent. Nearby, the old lock-house has recently been demolished to make way for a new reception centre next to an extensive restoration by the canal trust. This adjoins a new housing development and includes a reconstructed canal basin and wharf forming a fine pond of water. From here, the canal took a great sweep round Lassington Hill, coming close to the Newent road after a couple of miles.

The next lock was situated at Rudford and it is almost certainly the one recorded in the photograph reproduced on the cover of earlier editions of this book under the mistaken belief that the site was at Oxenhall. The error was eventually spotted after careful detective work by Brian Fox, and my only excuse is that the two locks and lock cottages did indeed look very much alike. But now, unlike the Oxenhall lock, the picture is changed utterly. Crossing a stile in a hedge there, who would believe that once it led directly onto a footbridge over a lock and to a cottage beyond, where generations of canal folk lived and died. And all that remains of this erstwhile scene, firstly a canal and then a railway, is an open field.

At Barber's Bridge the U-shaped canal formation, later occupied by the railway, is clearly visible from the road. W.P. Price had a private wharf here and occasionally full barge-loads of coal were unloaded. The sinuous wanderings began at Barber's Bridge, and a mile or so beyond, an isolated length of canal not used by the railway, can be seen from the old bridge on the lane to Moat Farm. Here, the long climb to Newent and Oxenhall tunnel commenced in earnest with a double or staircase lock, closely followed by another lock at Coneybury. The canal then crossed the Newent road and entered Road Lock near the site of the present abandoned railway bridge.

Passing close behind the Travellers' Rest, the canal crossed the Upleadon lane, and beyond this point its bed is now occupied by a private road as far as Okle Pitcher Mill, where there was also a lock. The old road to the mill is a disused grassy track leaving the main road a little past Upleadon Lane. The dried-up bed of the canal still lingers at the edge of a field north of the Newent bypass, where for most of its route, three modes of transport - canal, railway and road, have successively occupied the same stretch of ground. Near Cleeve Mill a lock lies buried; this was Newent lock where bargemen would at one time have passed within sight of Newent Spa, situated at the foot of a steep bank on the north side. The spa was never very successful, and an observer in 1852 reported, 'the well cottage a neat little building, is now untenanted and will soon present nothing but a ruin'.

Further west, the canal wove between two large ponds. One has long since been drained and its site bisected by the railway, and the other is Newent's ornamental lake, where a footpath runs by the dried-up bed and across a small aqueduct near the Newent bypass.

Newent wharf was on either side of the road to Dymock, and the basin is still visible in part, cut from solid rock behind the fire-station. Across the road a small dwelling, now much enlarged, was the office or wharf-house.

Originally, the canal passed beneath the road by means of a lift bridge. A permanent bridge later replaced it and when the railway came, the route was buried under many feet of embankment with the line crossing the road at high level. Several hundred yards beyond, the canal entered Devin's lock which was also destroyed by the railway. For the next few miles the routes diverged, leaving the canal undisturbed. Beyond Devin's lock it turned north and crossed the Ell Brook by a substantial aqueduct, still extant though in very poor repair. The footpath now crosses by a temporary iron bridge. After a stretch once more containing water, two more locks quickly followed, No. 2 and House lock, adjacent to Lock Cottage. The masonrywork of No. 2 has gone, but House lock, which represented the sole example on the whole canal to be seen in anything like its original state, is being completely restored by the trust. Lock Cottage is also fully restored and occupied and completes a delightful length of canal, a great amenity to the area.

The final lock for the next 6 miles was situated a little beyond, just past the Oxenhall-Three Ashes road, and for want of a proper name may be termed Top lock. Nearly all canals of any length boasted at least one branch, and if we include the tantalisingly brief Kilcot Coal Arm of the 1790s, the Hereford & Gloucester also qualifies. It commenced just beyond Top lock, and in the first edition I stated there was a gain in height of about 3 feet, implying a lock at the junction. In this, however, I was mistaken. A survey has shown no change in level, and should the Canal Trust ever decide to reinstate this intriguing and long forgotten relic of Newent's industrial dreams, its task will be that much the easier. It is also likely that the abutments of the original bridge over the branch still survive under the present road surface.

Of the branch itself, we are still able to distinguish a number of features, though all but a length recently cleared near Three Ashes Lane have long since been filled in. The route swung round below Oxenhall Church, where a steep bank borders the original line. To the west, the channel was again visible until about 1960 where it crossed a tributary of the Ell Brook, but now only the embankment and brick culvert remain. The final traces are south of White House. From the old tips of Newent Colliery (working in the 1870s) a footpath shown on Ordnance maps runs towards Lower House, and crosses a further brick culvert which carried the branch over the Brockmorehead stream. Beyond, a low rise in the ground and a shallow depression mark the last stretch as the canal approached Perkin's Hill House Colliery of 1796, which struggled on, with various intermissions, until the 1870s. It was the least unsuccessful of all the Newent pits. Years ago, when there was more of it to see, remnants of the branch indicated tight curves and a width somewhat under the usual 25 ft or so, in spite of its use by narrow-boats, which, by the by, Ballard termed 'long boats'. Here, it is worth mentioning that this latter designation was always the common one in Gloucestershire. The late Fred Rowbotham, with a lifetime's experience of local inland waterways, told me he had never heard of narrow boats until World War I.

As to Hill House Colliery itself, nothing now remains except for traces of coal in the banks of the brook. Indeed, none of this pastoral backwater of hedges and green fields reveals the least suggestion of an erstwhile scene of coalpits and pumping engines, colliers and engineers, and all the commotion of mining that for a few years represented the aspirations of the Herefordshire & Gloucestershire Canal Company, and its only real hope of profit.

Perkins & Moggridge also engaged in lime-burning, and although the scene of operations is uncertain, it may very well correspond to the remnants of a fine battery of kilns sacrificed for a bungalow in a quarry at Gorsley.

Returning to the junction, a transformation has taken place where not long ago the canal was overgrown and the towpath all but impassable. Clearance of scrub and dredging by both the landowner and the Canal Trust, though not as yet to the full width, has largely resurrected the scene as far as the notorious Oxenhall tunnel, much as it must have looked over a century ago. A restored towpath alongside the long reach of water beside Furnace Pond leads all the way to the bridge in Cold Harbour Lane, and to the tunnel. The bridge is typically Ballard, and probably replaced an earlier wooden bridge from the 1790s.

The tunnel portal has been restored, but such is the silting from the adjacent fields that after only a few years much of the dredging now needs doing again. Maintenance is an everlasting challenge for navigable waterways of every kind. Close by, is a peculiar chamber about 12 ft square in the solid rock, and the subject of much speculation. Reputedly a stable, it has also been restored by the Trust.

The 200-year-old Ellbrook aqueduct, now in very poor repair. A popular footpath runs along the towpath from Horsefair Lane past Lock Cottage and hence to Oxenhall tunnel.   *Author*

The Coal branch, looking towards the junction, 2001.   *Brian Fox*

The north end of Oxenhall tunnel about 1930. The portal has since collapsed and is now scarcely visible. *Author's Collection*

The south end, during restoration by the canal trust in 1998. *Brian Fox*

As earlier stated, construction of the tunnel gave rise to ruinous expense. Horse gins were brought from Sapperton tunnel on the Thames & Severn Canal, then recently completed, to assist in winding material from shafts sunk along the surface; a few grass-grown dumps still identify their sites. There were several in orcharding when I first visited the Boyce Court end 50 years ago; two dumps still survive near the M50.

When completed, the sections by no means fell into alignment, a circumstance which was verified by an officer of the Ordnance Survey, and confirmed by boatmen who described the tunnel as 'very crooked and very bad'. The Old Series one-inch maps published in 1831 indicate these deviations, but it is cautionary to observe that modern editions even on a large scale, mark the passage as a perfectly straight line.

In common with Sapperton, the luxury of a towpath through the tunnel was not provided - boats were legged through in the time-honoured fashion and horses walked over the hill. The cutting at the far end was long and deep, and hung with April daffodils must have been a glorious sight to boatmen after hours of dripping water, toil and darkness. At the tunnel, I am informed that boys would dive into the canal to retrieve coins that had slid out of the boatmen's pockets as they commenced to leg through.

At Boyce Court, once the home of the Moggridge family, the canal passed beneath a bridge similar to the one at the southern end of the tunnel, and a good stretch of water can still be seen from its parapet. To the west, the canal curved behind Dymock over a high embankment which the railway avoided. Further along it came close to the road, and Anchor House between the two, was once an inn to serve thirsty canal and turnpike travellers alike.

The formation is visible on either side of the private drive to Old Grange, and also in the form of a long embankment beyond the Dymock-Leominster road at

The wharfhouse on the Ross road at Ledbury, with extensions, about 1950. It is now enlarged and surrounded by modern developments.   *Author's Collection*

Windcross. The bridge which once spanned the canal at this point must have been extremely hump-backed, due to its situation on the very crest of a natural ridge of ground. Beyond, the railway has largely absorbed the route, and now in turn, also a memory.

About 1½ miles towards Ledbury at an isolated spot on the county boundary was Leather lock (the first since Oxenhall) and Leather Mill, scene of the 18th century steam pumping engine about which so very little is known. This tiny microcosm of industry and transport is now deserted and overgrown, and the mill itself reduced to a pathetic heap of rubble and timber. The Leadon was crossed by the aqueduct that blew out spectacularly in 1830, the site being indicated by abutments of the railway bridge. Another lock followed at Hazle Mill, now demolished, half a mile before the wharf on the Ross-Ledbury road which marked the terminus of the canal for over 30 years. The area is now the site of an industrial complex. Alongside the Ross road the considerably enlarged wharf-house is still occupied, but it was there before the canal came, and adapted for the purpose. A long brick shed nearby which served as a cider store was demolished some years ago, and claims that it had once been a barracks were never substantiated.

The wharf and summit level at Bye Street were gained by a flight of five deep locks later destroyed by the railway, where the route ascending through the town makes a splendid walk for local people. Here was the busy scene the young John Masefield knew, but of contemporary illustrations which must surely have existed, sadly none appear to survive.

The Ledbury-Hereford road and the Worcester-Hereford railway crossed the canal at the west end of Ledbury, where there was another wharf. A road bridge remains near Wellington Heath, and an embankment 25 feet high and ¼ mile long over the Leadon at Prior's Court formed the first major work on the extension. Within its tree-covered length are two aqueducts of ample dimensions, one crossing the River Leadon, the other for farm wagons to pass beneath. The canal could be isolated at the west end of the embankment by means of a half-lock or stop-gate, with a sluice for discharging water into the Leadon via a culvert. These features survive, though the timber of the gate is incomplete.

At Staplow on the Bosbury road, the wharf-house has been restored, but the adjacent bridge has long since been levelled. Beyond this point the canal followed a straight line across Swinmore Common before entering the long approach to Ashperton tunnel. Two fine bridges span the waters in the cutting but only the example near Moorend Farm is readily accessible.

Near Tunnel House, Ashperton tunnel provides one of the most impressive sights on the whole route. Here, the full depth of the cutting dug by pick and shovel is manifest, and we can well imagine the anxieties created by the continual slips during excavation. High above the tunnel portal, a solitary yew towering over a jungle of undergrowth deserves our notice. Early in the morning of 9th March, 1842, Stephen Ballard chose to plant this tree, an evergreen associated with ritual ever since prehistoric times, and bearing in mind his own final resting place, we may suspect the deed was not without a certain spiritual significance.

The derelict wharfhouse and outbuildings at Staplow in 1976, showing Ballard's influence in the design. The lean-to served as a butcher's shop. The house is now restored and occupied.   *Author*

Beyond, a line of grassy mounds denotes shafts, and two accommodation bridges span the deep cutting and a fine stretch of water. In this vicinity, old Ordnance maps indicate the sinuous nature of the route which was a product of the 1790s. The limited amount of work done here at the time included a bridge near the entrance to Canon Frome Court, and although it has been subsequently lowered, its style and narrow span are features that testify to an 18th century origin. The bridge once displayed ornamental embellishments in deference to the wishes of the Hopton family, and dating from a full half-century before a cargo-boat passed beneath it, is probably the oldest survivor on the canal. Two hundred yards towards Canon Frome, beneath a hump in the road ran the half-mile underground feeder from the River Frome. It emerged just to the right of the road, discharging into an open channel across the field to the canal. Both the tunnel mouth and the ditch have now been filled in, and only the hump remains in memory of a forgotten source of water that was sought for nearly 50 years.

Alongside the main road beyond Ashperton was the important wharf of Canon Frome. A wing has been added to the wharf-house where Ballard resided for a while, and it is worth remarking that nearly all the surviving wharf and lock-keepers houses have been enlarged over the years. The house and garden occupy built-up ground, and an orchard and lawn cover the site of the

A forgotten stretch of canal between Swinmore and Ashperton tunnel.   *Author*

An old postcard showing the canal and road bridge west of the tunnel. This section was completed in the 1790s.   *Author's Collection*

THE ITALIAN GATES, CANON FFROME COURT, NR. LEDBURY.

Above: Tunnel House, Ashperton, before restoration. It stands on the very edge of the deep cutting leading to the tunnel, below.   *Author's Collection*

Right: The heavily silted east end of Ashperton tunnel in 1977; inside, the towpath is under water.   *Author*

wharf. One of the two warehouses built into the wharf can be seen from the road.

Canon Frome Wharf marked the commencement of the long embankment over the Frome Valley, much of which has been removed apart from an undisturbed section north of the Yarkhill road. To the west is Monksbury Mill, once driven by the River Lodon and the object of much discussion in the 1790s as a water supply. Farther along at Monkhide a long stretch of canal has been restored by the Canal Trust, and includes four bridges with Ballard's famous skew bridge in pride of place. Further canal buildings are at Crew's Pitch Wharf alongside the Worcester-Hereford road, beyond which restoration is partly completed as far as Barr's lock, unfortunately long since destroyed.

In a very isolated spot, Barr's lock marked the end of the 10 mile summit level, and then followed a wharf and cottage at the Kymin. Two more locks about a mile apart brought the canal down to its final level, the last being adjacent to the road north of Withington. It is now filled in as part of the garden of the lock-keeper's house. The road bridge bears the date 1843, but in contrast to Ballard's usual style, its design is very cramped without even a towpath.

In a further mile Withington Wharf was reached, and the site now exhibits the largest group of canal buildings on the route. On the road to Sutton St Nicholas a typical bridge survives, although the channel is filled in.

The long embankment that crossed the valley of the Lugg has been badly cut about, and in places has vanished without trace, though a bridge still takes a cart track over the dried-up channel. From Shelwick Green towards Hereford the route is visible in places, and the Roman road to Holmer crosses it via the new bridge, stone from the old bridge having been donated by the Highway Authority and used in rebuilding the lock at Oxenhall.

In a corner of Holmer Trading Estate, opposite the Bridge Inn, the entrance to Aylestone tunnel is now almost buried in rubbish, although at the time of an earlier visit daylight could be discerned at the far end, which emerges in the grounds of a factory. For the next half-mile the route swung eastwards and has been obliterated. The canal passed under a bridge at the junction of Mortimer Road and Burcott Road, and a noticeable hump in the road denotes a bridge long since buried below. A little beyond, Burcott Road and the canal passed side by side beneath the Shrewsbury-Hereford Railway. Further on, the construction of two new bridges at a trading development have safeguarded the canal's approach to the city, as has been mentioned in the previous chapter.

Another half-mile brought the canal to its destination at Barr's Court. Nothing now remains of the wharves or buildings, and the final remnant is rather unprepossessing bridge which has been widened, probably in the 1870s, at the northern end of Widemarsh Street. There are iron railings on one side and the whole is supported on cast-iron beams mainly buried in brickwork.

So much for the Hereford & Gloucester Canal after more than a century's abandonment. As for the future, with the old vision of the 1790s resurrected in the form of the canal trust, the final chapter in the story of this beautiful waterway is still being written.

Two of the three canal arms at Hereford about 50 years ago.   *(Both) Author's Collection*

Chapter Ten

Stephen Ballard
1804-1890

Where the old road from Ledbury begins its steep climb over the Malvern Hills an arboretum-like quality becomes apparent in the surroundings; stately and exotic trees abound, and the traveller senses that he is traversing the grounds of a carefully planned and landscaped estate. To the right, above a private drive that contours round the hill is a clump of pines on a grassy mound like some prehistoric tomen, a feature which calls for no particular notice except that the tump is formed of waste from a railway tunnel, and among its soil is the grave of Stephen Ballard. The tunnel was his creation, and it was in keeping with the man's nature that when the time came, unconsecrated ground on his own estate should provide his final resting place.

Stephen Ballard was born on 5th April, 1804 at Ivy House on Malvern Link Common, the fifth of seven children of Philip and Charlotte Ballard. Both parents came of Herefordshire stock, his mother being a Baylis of Ledbury. The father rose to the position of attorney, but an inclination to drink so strained his resources that only the thrift and industry of his wife in accommodating paying guests saved the family from insolvency.

Stephen Ballard's school days consisted of a series of indifferent and even thoroughly bad establishments that then frequently masqueraded under the name of education. He finally absconded from the College School, Worcester, taking up the care of his father's sheep and gardening at the family home. Whilst in the latter occupation, he was noticed by the dowager Marchioness of Donegal, then resident at Ivy House, who found him a post in Lea and Kennedy's nurseries at Hammersmith. He commenced in 1822, later moving to Earl Plymouth's Hewell Grange near Bromsgrove. Ballard however, was not content with the limited scope of horticulture, and after declining the offer of a position at Kew Gardens procured by the kindly dowager, he became apprenticed on 6th May, 1825 to Henry Lucy,* a builder of Cheltenham. Lucy generously allowed a wage of 12s. per week in the first year, and the grounding which he received in carpentry and masonrywork proved of great value. A slump in Lucy's affairs cut short the apprenticeship but a few months later, on 13th August, 1827 Ballard at the age of 23 became appointed Clerk to the Herefordshire & Gloucestershire Canal Navigation Company under circumstances already described.

Ballard's enthusiasm for his new post made a great impression, and in the summer of 1829 he was given £25 for a fact-finding visit to the Liverpool & Manchester Railway, then under construction. He set out on 20th June and on the way inspected the Shropshire Union & Ellesmere Canals, including Telford's famous Pontcystlle aqueduct near Llangollen. Slate quarries near Bangor and the Menai and Conway bridges were also examined, and at Liverpool he walked 10 miles along the railway accompanied by 'Mr

---

* Lucy became agent to the Gloucester & Cheltenham horse-tramroad in 1834. See the author's *Gloucester & Cheltenham Railway*, Oakwood Press, 1987. Ballard never forgot his old master and often put business in his path.

Stephen Ballard, 1804-1890.

Stephen Ballard's birthplace, Ivy House at Malvern Link as seen in 1998.

Sinclair Johnston

Stephenson the Engineer'. The tour concluded with visits to the Duke of Bridgewater's Canal, the Rochdale Canal and others in the area.

Back in Ledbury, he was soon working on the idea of lock gates constructed wholly of oak to avoid the decay created by the use of iron bolts - an idea which was put into practice and on 25th February, 1831 he rode in Goldsworthy Gurney's steam coach operating its short-lived service between Gloucester and Cheltenham.

During a spell in London in the autumn of 1834 Ballard visited factories including Gordon's chain-cable works at Deptford, and took the opportunity of presenting to Mr Milne of the Office of Woods and Forests a copy of a book on pruning which he had recently written. He was in fact a great anti-pruner. 'I never pass on the road between Newent and Gloucester without deploring the miserable state of the timber trees and the great ignorance of the nature of trees that their owners display by mutilating them as they do'. In 1836, an ambitious plan arose in the form of the Severn Navigation Company for adapting the river for ocean-going vessels as far as Worcester by means of locks, weirs and new channels wherever necessary. Thomas Rhodes was appointed engineer in charge and a great deal of work confronted him prior to submitting proposals for Parliamentary approval. Rhodes had worked on the Caledonian Canal and the Menai Bridge under Thomas Telford, and two of the master's finest works, the bridge of iron at the Mythe, Tewkesbury, and one of stone at Over, were to provide frequent reminders of his associations with that great engineer.

The Herefordshire & Gloucestershire committee was not adverse to Ballard gaining experience by accepting extra duties where time permitted, and for 12 months following April 1836, he worked almost continuously under Rhodes preparing surveys and plans, and taking recordings of river sections and velocities. For a time he lived in rooms at 2 College Church Yard, Worcester, before moving to 7, Summer Place. The job entailed long hours in all weathers, but even at weekends with a chance of relaxation, Ballard would think nothing of walking to Malvern on the Saturday evening, to Ledbury and back on Sunday, and returning to Worcester in time for work next day - a total distance of nearly 30 miles.

Another of Rhodes' assistants was Edward Leader Williams, who had an ironmonger's shop in Worcester. Williams learnt the art of surveying from Ballard on the banks of the river, and later rose to eminence as engineer to the Severn Commission. His son became a famous landscape artist, painting under the name of Edward Williams Leader.

Stephen Ballard often lodged at the Star Inn at Upton-on-Severn, the House in the Tree (now the Bridge Inn) at Haw Bridge, and the Dog at Over (now the Toby Carvery).

In the latter vicinity he was acquainted with the Murrell family, and one Sunday 'took supper there and spent a very pleasant evening - the two Miss Murrells very lively good humoured tolerably good looking girls - was much pleased with their company'.

A few days later, in November 1836 whilst engaged in surrepticious surveying on the estate of Apperley Court he had a difficult encounter with Miss Strickland and her bailiff, but the latter 'softened down much by my talking to him' - an example of Ballard's tact and diplomacy which stood him in such good stead with stubborn landowners on the line of the Herefordshire & Gloucestershire Canal.

During the autumn he was introduced to James Walker and William Cubitt of the Institution of Civil Engineers, of which he shortly afterwards became an Associate Member. At the end of 1836 a week was spent in Wales surveying the Llanelly Railway in the Loughor Valley at the instigation of John Biddulph of Ledbury. His son, John Biddulph junior, was concerned in the project and had commercial interests including a colliery in the area.

Throughout his long life Ballard displayed considerable talent as an inventor and two very contrasting ideas, the fruits of 1836, occupied much of his attention. One achieved wide acclaim, and won for its originator the Institution of Civil Engineers' Telford Medal. It concerned an improved ice-breaking machine, the principle of which he confided to Thomas Rhodes on 18th August of that year; as with all great inventions the concept was simplicity itself. The plan involved cracking the ice from below instead of above, and virtually reversed the old system; a prototype was launched from Ledbury Wharf on 20th December, 1837 and three weeks later eight boats were liberated on the first working trial to Over.

In January 1838 Ballard observed 'at Dymock ice 4 inches thick broken with ease, only drawn by 2 weak horses', and a fortnight afterwards four horses managed to break 9 inches. Some years later, on 1st February 1845 an ice-boat made of iron was tried which 'answered uncommon well, breaking ice 2 in. thick with only a weak old Horse, a man to steer and a man to drive'.

In the severe winters of the 19th century the importance of the invention to canal proprietors could hardly be over-estimated, and it found wide adoption in this country as well as abroad, probably with little or no financial reward for its originator. There are full details of the invention in *The Wharfinger*, No. 64.

The other idea of 1836 ended in failure notwithstanding Ballard's pursuit of the goal on and off for many years. Whilst walking from Malvern to Worcester through a field of wheat stubble the concept dawned upon him of destroying weeds by forcing a flame onto the ground by a fan driven from the axle of a two-wheeled machine, the flame being generated from coal or other fuel. 'May be drawn by a stubborn horse', noted Ballard in an uncharacteristic display of humour, 'and the more stubborn he is the nearer he should be hooked to the fire'.

He was soon making experiments on the 'scorcher', and in May 1839 Messrs Jones and Draper of Witney expressed an interest, having seen the machine described in a Leeds newspaper. At a meeting in Cheltenham they produced 'a very ingenious model made in mahogany, brass and copper'. This led to a full sized version which it was proposed to patent, somewhat late in the day however, in view of the prior publicity, and there the project seems to have rested. As late as 1862 the still optimistic inventor recorded 'tried an experiment with my Scorcher, found no difficulty in getting a very fierce flame against the ground . . . No doubt the time will come when it will be the most useful of all agricultural implements'.

We must now return to the spring of 1837, when Ballard broke off associations with the Severn Navigation just before its Bill was rejected by Parliament. He then became introduced to the Dowdeswells of Pull Court near Tewkesbury, and undertook construction of a reservoir and water supply to the house, and also a new carriage road to Bushley Green.

In May 1837, he set off by coach with his brother Philip for further work on the Llanelly Railway. The task took about three weeks and they occupied a cottage at Llangenrock near Pontardulais, 'very dirty and with scarcely any furniture'. The mining region of Wales did not appeal to Ballard, with its Cross Inn at Ynestonlog 'a filthy place filled with drunken men and women'. He was glad to return to Ledbury, but later complained bitterly of the company's refusal to meet more than £50 of his £79 fee. Philip Ballard was a very capable artist and assisted in preparing plans and estimates for the line. Afterwards, more jobs developed at Pull Court, with discussions about draining Longdon Marsh, concerning which Dowdeswell produced papers going back over a hundred years.

Interspersed with these activities was work on an intended railway from Droitwich to the Worcester & Birmingham Canal, and later in the year the brothers were busy surveying the proposed canal extension from Ledbury to Hereford, also the River Lugg to Leominster. The task concluded on 21st April, 1837, and Ballard ended the day by walking home from Leominster - a distance of 22 miles. 'Not much tired' he recorded. Feats such as these occasioned little comment in days before the motor car.

Almost since the beginning of his canal appointment, Stephen Ballard had shared a house at Ledbury with his older brother Robert, and following the latter's marriage in February 1839 he seriously considered buying a home of his own. But John Biddulph, with a fatherly interest in his career, advised against a fixed place of residence other than London, and in the end Ballard moved to a house in South Parade, Ledbury. Soon afterwards his salary was raised to £400 annually, a sum no less than one quarter of the canal's annual revenue. At this time he also took on his first apprentice, Samuel Willcox. The lad walked 17 miles from Gloucester with his father and Ballard recorded how he broke down at the sight of his father commencing the long journey home.

Although construction of the canal occupied Ballard almost exclusively, over the next few years he became increasingly concerned about a future vocation, and was advised by W.P. Price to concentrate on railways which were rapidly growing in importance. However, in the event, he accepted the promise of the Resident Engineer's post under James Walker on the Middle-Level Main Drain in the Fens, an arrangement which his old company endorsed provided he continued to support their interests.

When Stephen Ballard reached Kings Lynn on 25th May, 1845, one of his first actions was to send for Sam Willcox to come as an assistant and a companion. The works occupied about two years, and the interlude proved for the most part an unhappy one. Disagreements frequently arose with Walker and there were many recurrences of the severe headaches to which he had long been prone. This was a family tendency attributed to low blood pressure, which fortunately ameliorated with passing years. In addition he found the local people distant and unsociable, only the occasional journey to old haunts relieving his loneliness.

During this period, Ballard made proposals for new docks at Gloucester in conjunction with W.P. Price and Causton the surveyor. At the former's instigation he approached I.K. Brunel for a situation and received a favourable response. 'Mr Brunell [sic] was willing to engage me', he recorded, 'I wrote and said I was willing if the salary would suit but do not feel inclined to go to him for less than £800 a year'. Nothing materialised, and in December 1845 he received news that his mother to whom he was much attached, was gravely ill. She died a few weeks later, and to add to his distress there were 'the very worst accounts possible from Ledbury' concerning trade on the canal.

After a further year, events took a turn for the better. At that time Thomas Brassey, the railway contractor, was building the Great Northern Railway from London to Peterborough, and it was almost inevitable that the two men would meet. Brassey had heard of Ballard's work on drainage, and wished to learn of his ideas for constructing an embankment across a mile or more of floating bog 25 ft deep at Whittlesea Mere. Their first discussion took place on 27th March, 1847.

Brassey, a year younger, had also begun in the building trade and exhibited a similar reserved and unassuming disposition, with a tremendous capacity for work. An affinity sprang up, and a few months later the terms of Ballard's employment were resolved. He wanted £800 yearly, but settled for £500 plus a share of the profits. This was at Brassey's suggestion and made Ballard a great deal of money, sufficient in fact for him to retire, not, however, that he did so.

Carrying the line over the bog was effected by his plan of lowering the water table and laying down a multiple sandwich of hurdles, faggots and peat to prevent the material dispersing in a lateral direction.

During this period Ballard became acquainted with John Bird, a farmer through whose land the line passed on the edge of the Mere. Here, at least, was a welcome for Bird's daughter, then a girl of 18 or 19 years, was to become his wife.

From this point lengthy gaps appear in his diaries, though it is clear that he was a very close associate of Brassey, the partnership of Brassey & Ballard soon becoming a household name. In the summer of 1851 he spent a few months in India, and later in the year the two men were involved in a scheme for a projected sea-level canal across the isthmus of Panama. The task of making the survey was delegated to Ballard, but in the meantime he spent several weeks in Holland in connection with the Rhenish Railway. He visited Antwerp, Arnhem, Utrecht and Rotterdam but all the while was uneasy about the impending mission to Panama, and in the end turned it down.

Then, in July 1852 whilst engaged with Willcox in Ireland on drainage schemes at Tramore, a letter was received from Brassey with a request to take charge of a large contract involving construction of 100 miles of the Grand Trunk Railway of Canada. Again, he could feel events slipping beyond control by the consequences of his own success. 'If I had ten times as much time', he had written in the canal days, 'I could spend it all on the works which I take pleasure in'. But circumstances had changed. In the Fens he had complained that everything tended to wean him from Herefordshire and now, less in command than 20 years before, there arose the probability of long assignments in the New World.

Although sharing Brassey's faith in the value of railways to society, Ballard's roots in the old country, and the three counties in particular, were proving too strong. He had recently acquired a small estate at Colwall and in addition matrimony was in the air.

My mind has been much engaged considering this offer to go to Canada [he confided]. Mr Brassey advises me to think seriously of it or I believe I should at once have declined; 100 miles will probably take 5 years to complete. Can I make up my mind to leave England & all friends for so long a time. My place at Colwall of which I am fond, not yet completed sufficiently for me to leave it without loss, or at least not having the work done exactly to my mind & as yet decidedly inclined to marry . . .will not this interfere with this important event and perhaps prevent it? Of course the inducement for me to give up all these prospects must be very great .

Two days later Ballard declined the offer, and a fortnight afterwards set sail for further work at Tramore. Brassey took the refusal in good part, and therefore excursions were in the main confined to France and the Low Countries where his skills practised in the Fens were put to good use. As it happened, he was well out of the venture which proved fraught with difficulties and little short of disastrous for Brassey.

Stephen Ballard married Maria Bird in 1854, and after two years in Holland they made their home at his new farm, the Winnings at Colwall, where eight children were eventually born. Her name, Maria Ballard, lives on in a boat belonging to Major R.E. Barnes.

Two rare booklets by Stephen Ballard on subjects dear to his heart, and published half a century apart.

Ballard's early portable engine of uncertain origin, retired among Colwall daffodils in 1977. It has since been acquired by a steam enthusiast.   *Author*

In 1856 the old idea of a line from Worcester to Hereford was successfully promoted, and Ballard gained a contract for construction in association with Thomas Brassey. The opening of the railway through the tunnel under the Malverns to Colwall station called for celebrations at the farm, and the festivities coincided with a trainload of coal provided by the two contractors arriving for the poor of the parish.

During the next five or six years Ballard was mainly involved with new lines in the West Midlands, including the Evesham & Ashchurch, Evesham & Redditch, Worcester & Bromyard, and the ill-fated East Gloucestershire Railway. He acted as agent and contractor for both the Evesham lines, but lost money on both. His last undertaking, again in conjunction with Brassey, was the extension of the Midland Railway from Bedford to London, commenced in 1865.

Thereafter Ballard chose increasingly to breath his native air on his own ground, where his love of agricultural pursuits could be indulged to the full. He was an early exponent of steam ploughing, and erected a fixed engine in a shed with a windlass, and a pulley placed in the field. He practised this system for 30 years, and his farm buildings (which still survive, although used for other purposes) were considered models of their kind.

Influenced no doubt by memories of childhood, Ballard was always teetotal and about 1880 he built a Temperance Hotel and Workmen's Hall. He was also prime mover and constructor of the fine high level 'Jubilee Drive' that contours the west flanks of the Malvern Hills, and gave a considerable portion of the necessary land. Many old workmen and colleagues visited him at the Winnings, and his first apprentice, Samuel Willcox, who had married his niece Mary Spencer, came to live nearby at The Grange, Bosbury. Further details of Willcox's career are to be found in C. Walker's, *Thomas Brassey, Railway Builder* 1969.

Ballard maintained a great interest in transport matters and strongly supported the principle of light railways; his booklet *Cheap Railways for Rural Districts* was first published in 1884, and went to two editions. Also in 1884 he established a vinegar works at Colwall, and the buildings are still to be seen in the village. In addition, he constructed a number of houses with walls made of concrete, which also survive in the area.

Stephen Ballard was of a public-spirited disposition, and largely due to his efforts the Malvern Hills are an outstanding area of recreation, an amenity which is nowadays rather taken for granted. By the late 1870s the local population was growing rapidly, and legal remedy could not readily deter land encroachments that were assuming alarming proportions. Indeed, short of drastic action the eventual loss to the public of the whole area of common seemed inevitable.

Fortunately, as a result of several public meetings, Ballard and Professor Raper of Trinity College, Oxford, drafted a Bill which became law in 1884, establishing a Board of Conservators with a power of summary jurisdiction. As an example of the problem, over 100 encroachments were dealt with in the first year, and a further Act was obtained in 1924. Subsequently, the conservators bought up mineral rights to restrict quarrying, and so prevented the Malverns in great measure from literally disappearing.

As an alternative to open quarrying, Ballard suggested the idea of mining the stone and thus incidentally, enabling a road to be formed through the hills. He had in fact proposed a tunnel as early as 1836, but the scheme never materialised.

Stephen Ballard combined a modest and unassuming disposition with a generous nature, but in spite of great drive and perserverance was inclined to hide his light under a bushel. However, he never underestimated his worth to an employer. He was outspoken against capital punishment and blood sports, and held social beliefs that were generally ahead of the times. As an example of his compassion we may cite the following example in dealing with a contractor on the canal extension to Hereford in 1840. 'Holland has been at work for a month but on measuring up there was nothing to come to him. He was in great trouble and offered me his watch if I would lend him £4. I would not take it, but advanced him the money which I expect he will never repay'.

Ballard's views were on the whole radical and somewhat puritanical. He had no unquestioning regard for social superiors. 'Sir Thomas Warmington sat in the little room with us for some time and behaved very agreeably, not at all like the generality of gentlemen. He is a plain straightforward man'.

From first to last Ballard was a child of the country, and in an age when religious beliefs were strong, his faith lay closer to nature; his diaries constantly reveal an affinity with the natural world - 'Thrushes singing beautifully at Frampton', 'tried to save the Ash Tree that has the mistletoe growing in it', 'Swifts arrived at Ledbury, saw them for the first time this season early in the morning of this day'.

In an age when one man could command almost absolute control of a large enterprise and stand or fall by the outcome, Ballard's utter dedication to work is easy to understand. In our day, endless authorities and committees retard progress interminably, and insulate one and all from retribution or acclaim. Much as we may deplore it, there can be no leaders in the old mould now.

Chapter Eleven

The Gloucester-Ledbury Railway
by John Norris

When it finally happened, the closure of the Hereford & Gloucester Canal so that a railway might be built upon much of its bed was not without an ironical overtone, for only the old route was converted and not the extension that had been in great measure constructed with just such a project in mind.

How this finally came about had its origins as early as 1872, when plans were published for two undertakings, - the Ross & Ledbury Railway and the Newent Railway. The Ross & Ledbury was projected to connect the places named in its title, passing through Dymock and connecting at Ross with both the Hereford & Gloucester and Ross & Monmouth lines, in all about 12½ miles. With its connection with the Worcester & Hereford facing towards Worcester, it would have permitted direct running between Worcester and Monmouth and so might be regarded as a successor to the railway proposed some 10 years earlier.

The Newent Railway was to join the GWR at Over, passing through Newent to join the Ross & Ledbury at Dymock, a distance of about 12 miles. The two railways were separately incorporated in 1873. The Ross & Ledbury was empowered to make extensive use of the canal north of Dymock for its line, while the Newent Railway also took powers to use much of the canal, intending also to convert Oxenhall tunnel to its use; the latter plan was changed, however, and powers to build a length of line to avoid the tunnel were obtained in 1874.

A leading figure in both undertakings was Michael Biddulph, grandson of John Biddulph, who had been active in furthering the canal interests more than 50 years before. George Clive of Perrystone and William Partridge of Wyelands, both near Ross-on-Wye, were also leading figures in the Ross & Ledbury company; the latter was a Director of the Ross & Monmouth Railway. The whole of the initial capital was subscribed by these men and others who may well have been business associates, although the presence among them of John William Miles, a Director of the GWR, suggests that he was there to watch the interests of that company. Little or no attempt seems to have been made to raise the remainder of the capital and in 1876 the GWR agreed to provide the whole of the capital needed by both companies. Thereupon, both the existing Boards of Directors retired and were replaced by GWR nominees with Sir Daniel Gooch as Chairman. As far as the Ross & Ledbury was concerned, the GWR could see no justification for the line between Ross and Dymock, limiting its financial support for the section from there to Ledbury.

The GWR was in no hurry to proceed and it was not until the summer of 1881 that construction work began southwards from Ledbury, thus enabling the canal to be used for the conveyance of materials from the Severn. Early in 1883 construction work began from Dymock towards Newent. From Ledbury to Dymock a double track was laid, so providing for the additional traffic if the line to Ross were ever built. A single track only was laid from Dymock to Over, although the works allowed for doubling. Stations were provided at Dymock (regarded as part of the Newent Railway), Newent itself and Barber's Bridge

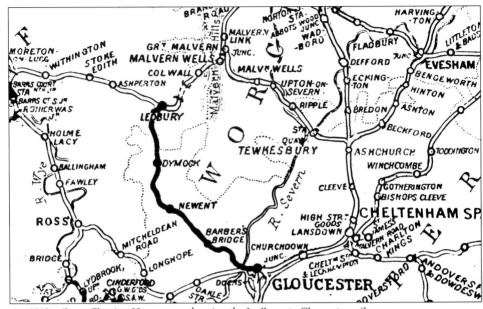

1913 railway Clearing House map showing the Ledbury to Gloucester railway.

This imposing bridge under the Worcester-Hereford line at Ledbury arose from visions of turning the canal into a railway; ironically, only the 18th century section from Gloucester was ever thus converted. To the west is a fine viaduct built by Robert Ballard from bricks made on the spot.   *Author*

and each had crossing facilities. The contractors throughout were Messrs Appleby & Lawton and the signalling was carried out by Messrs McKenzie & Holland, the well-known firm of signalling engineers of Worcester. The total outlay on the two undertakings was almost £269,000 including £35,000 for the proprietors of the canal company.

At last all was ready and on Monday 27th July, 1885, without ceremony, a public service commenced to coincide with the summer show of the Gloucestershire Agricultural Society. Initially there were five passenger trains each way between Gloucester and Ledbury on weekdays only, all running through to or from Malvern or Worcester. Some of these trains were worked by a locomotive which stabled at the small shed near the GWR station at Malvern Wells. While strikes and war-time conditions caused services to be curtailed from time to time, the initial frequency was the pattern for much of the life of the line. Sunday services seem never to have been a feature of the timetables. For travel between Gloucester and Hereford, the route via Ledbury was a recognised alternative to that via Ross-on-Wye. One local goods train was also provided on weekdays.

The line gave a shorter route from Gloucester to the Birmingham district than had been previously available to the GWR, offering a valuable saving in mileage compared with the route via Hereford. Accordingly, through freight workings to Worcester and Stourbridge were introduced, to be followed by others to Bordesley Junction and Wolverhampton. To handle this traffic, the signal boxes at Newent and Dymock remained open continuously on weekdays; at Barber's Bridge, however, the box was closed at night and an unusual arrangement allowed freight trains and light engines to pass through the station towards Gloucester on the wrong road with the signals at danger and the lights in the signal lamps extinguished.

The opening of the North Warwickshire line on 9th December, 1907, completed the new main line of the GWR between Gloucester and Birmingham via Stratford-upon-Avon, and with it there was an extensive revision, all but one of the through freight services via Newent being diverted to the new route.

Although these changes had reduced the value of the line as a through route, this was the time when the country railway was in its heyday, and Newent enjoyed facilities which can only surprise us today. Passengers' luggage in advance could be collected or delivered at addresses in the town, while the firm of R.T. Smith & Co. operated a railway parcels receiving office, additional to that at the station.

Agricultural and other requirements of the district often required special services. Timetables provided for cattle trains to be run to Gloucester for the market, if required, on two days a week, while arrangements had to be made for the handling of seasonal fruit traffic, usually sent via Ledbury to Worcester, to be forwarded to northern markets with produce from elsewhere in the Midlands. It is also on record that, in connection with the Royal Agricultural Society's show held at Clifton Down, Bristol, in 1913, a special train for livestock called at both Dymock and Newent on its way from Worcester to Clifton; after the show the line appears to have been opened specially on a Sunday for the passage of a return train which stopped at Dymock to set down a horse, a mare and a foal.

Excursion trains from the Midlands to South Wales and the West Country also called at stations on the line over many years. On a Sunday in June 1936 strangers

Two period postcard views of Dymock station, viewed from the road bridge. Only a length of platform survives to resurrect the scenes.   *John Alsop Collection and Author's Collection*

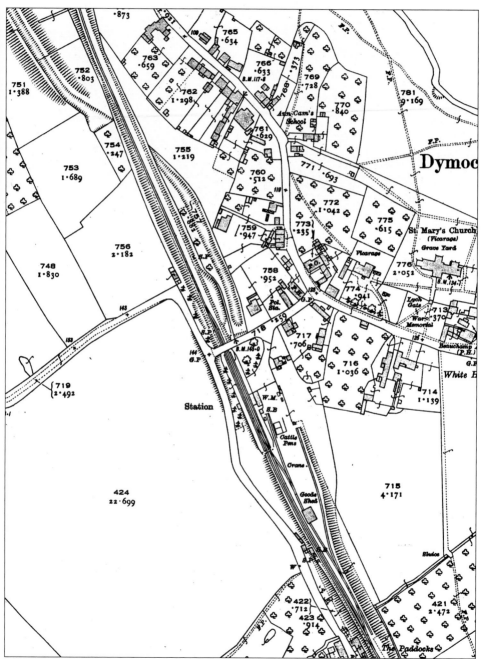

Dymock station showing the railway and part of the formation of the canal (*top*).
Reproduced from the 25", 1923 Ordnance Survey Map

Dymock station on 7th December, 1963. The site has since been developed though the road bridge, hidden by steam, remains.

B.J. Ashworth

BR 2-6-0 No 78006 from Dymock gains the summit at Four Oaks Halt on 21st December, 1963. This deep cutting is now filled in, with only a bridge parapet remaining.   *B.J.Ashworth*

This 1873 Parliamentary plan of the proposed railway shows its course obliterating the canal and wharf (No. 42) at Newent. Note: North is pointing downwards.   *Author's Collection*

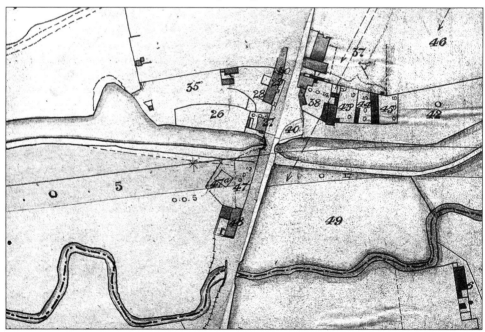

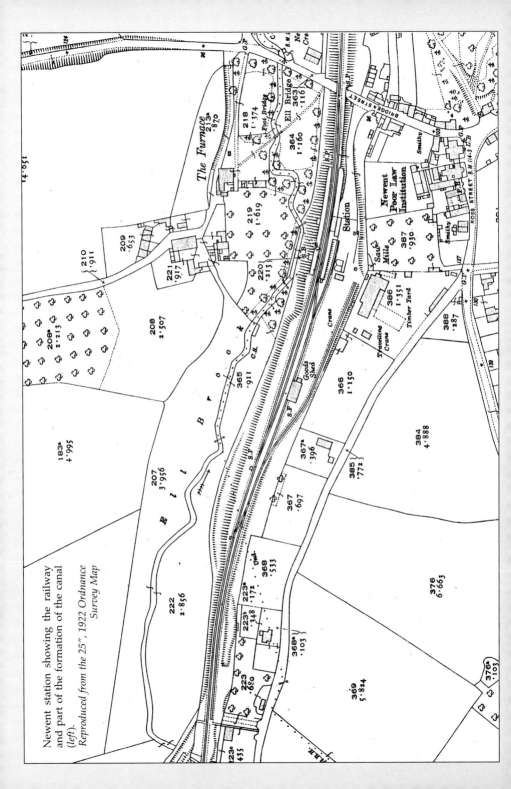

Newent station showing the railway
and part of the formation of the canal
(*left*).
*Reproduced from the 25", 1922 Ordnance
Survey Map*

A period postcard view of Newent station. *John Alsop Collection*

Ex-GWR 0-4-2 tank engine No. 1427 on a Ledbury train at Newent one spring morning in 1959.
Note the token being handed to the driver to enable the train to proceed. *Author*

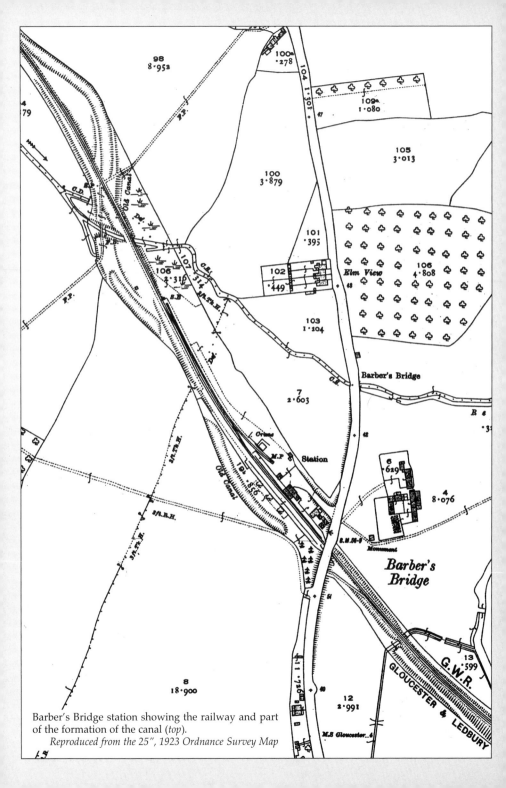

Barber's Bridge station showing the railway and part
of the formation of the canal (*top*).
Reproduced from the 25", 1923 Ordnance Survey Map

A view of Barber's Bridge station on 5th December, 1963 with a freight train from Gloucester to Dymock, hauled by Collett 0-6-0 No. 2291. This is the sole station remaining, with the foreground now a garden. *B.J. Ashworth*

Collett 0-6-0 No. 2232 heads north, with a short goods train, a mile south-east of Barber's Bridge station on 24th January, 1962. The River Leadon can be seen in the background. *B.J. Ashworth*

0-6-0 pannier tank No. 8717 takes water at Gloucester Central on the 9th June, 1959, prior to departing with the 4.08 pm train to Ledbury. *B.J. Ashworth*

Can you spot the mistake on this plaque, on the site of the Newent by-pass? *Author*

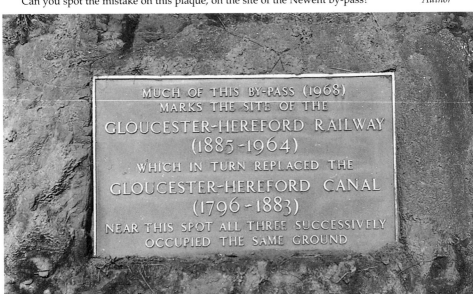

were received in the form of LMSR trains between Gloucester and Birmingham, diverted from their own line because of engineering work near Gloucester.

In May 1892 the line played a small part in a notable piece of railway history. A special train conveying gangers ran from Chipping Norton Junction (now Kingham) via Cheltenham and Newent to Ledbury, there to join others on their way to assist in the conversion of the broad gauge from Exeter to Truro; seven men from the Newent area were among them.

The inevitable search for operating economies began early. In 1895, as the result of available connections towards Worcester, one passenger train from Gloucester was terminating at Ledbury, and by the summer of 1898 a second such working had been introduced. Also in 1898 the signal box at Barber's Bridge was closed, the crossing loop taken out and the down bay platform abandoned. In 1916 the double-line section between Dymock and Ledbury was singled, and in the summer of 1918 the remaining through passenger trains between Gloucester and Worcester were withdrawn, leaving a purely local service to run between Gloucester and Ledbury.

Commencing in 1940, passenger services were given over to a diesel railcar based at Cheltenham. However, for a period in the 1950s the car was used on a morning run from Gloucester to Birmingham and back via Stratford-upon-Avon, leaving two round trips on the Newent line to be worked by a steam push-and-pull train.

In an attempt to encourage increased passenger use of the railway, four halts were opened, each having a short wooden platform and a simple shelter. These were:

Malswick	1st February, 1938
Four Oaks	16th October, 1937
Greenway	1st April, 1937
Ledbury Town	26th November, 1928

After World War II, inter-availability of rail and bus tickets was introduced between Gloucester and Newent. On the freight side, the GWR was active between the wars in the development of country lorry services for the collection and delivery of consignments at farms and outlying premises, and such services were available at both Newent and Dymock.

But in common with other country railways, the heyday of the line from Gloucester to Ledbury largely disappeared after World War I as rural life fell increasingly under the influence of the car, the lorry and the omnibus, and electricity displaced coal as a source of heat and power. The last passenger trains ran on 11th July, 1959, after which the section between Ledbury and Dymock closed completely. The three intermediate stations remained open for freight traffic until the end of May 1964, and thus there came to an end the life of a railway which had served the community for nearly 79 years.

There were, however, signs of a revival in 1989, when a local paper announced that the Leadon Valley Electric Railway Association was to apply for a Light Railway Order to relay the line for tramcars. Amongst other difficulties, how both a restored railway and canal were to share a common route was never explained, and not surprisingly this delightful dream has faded into oblivion.

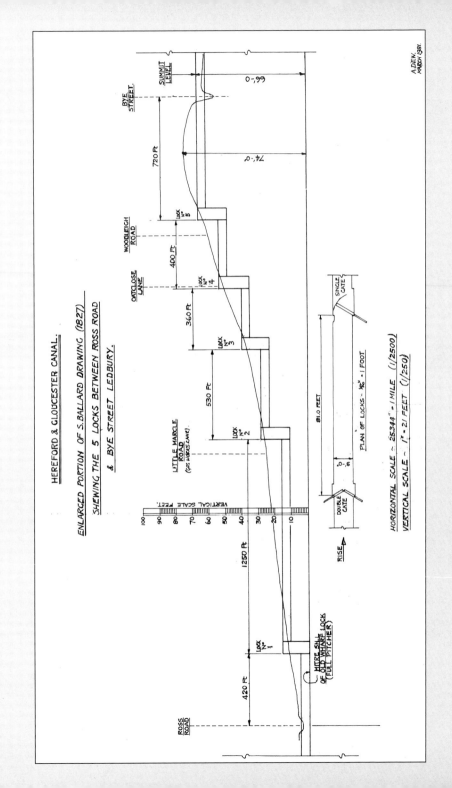

HEREFORD & GLOUCESTER CANAL.

ENLARGED PORTION OF S.BALLARD DRAWING (1827)

SHEWING THE 5 LOCKS BETWEEN ROSS ROAD & BYE STREET LEDBURY.

SUMMIT LEVEL

BYE STREET

0.99

74'-0"

720 Ft

LOCK No 5

WOODLEIGH ROAD

400 Ft

OATCLOSE LANE

LOCK No 4

360 Ft

LOCK No 3

LITTLE MARCLE ROAD (GAS WORKS LANE)

530 Ft

LOCK No 2

VERTICAL SCALE FEET.

100 90 80 70 60 50 40 30 20 10

1250 Ft

LOCK No 1

420 Ft

ROSS ROAD

MITRE SILL OF OLD WHARF LOCK (FULL PITCHER)

SINGLE GATE

81.0 FEET

PLAN OF LOCKS ~ ½" = 1 FOOT

9'-0"

DOUBLE GATE

RISE

HORIZONTAL SCALE ~ 25.344" = 1 MILE (1/2500)

VERTICAL SCALE ~ 1" = 21 FEET (1/250)

A.DEW. MARCH 1981.

Appendix One

Locks on the Hereford & Gloucester Canal

18th Century Construction

19th Century Construction

Name	Grid Reference	Name	Grid reference
Over Lock	817198	* Wharf Lock	703369
* Rudford Lock	781214	* --	+
* Double Locks	755243	* --	+
* Coneybury Lock	752244	* --	+
* Road Lock	748248	* --	+
* Philip's Lock	738259	Barr's Lock	597448
* Newent Lock	731262	Thingwell Lock	581448
* Devin's Lock	715264	Withington Lock	567441
No. 2 Lock	713265		
House Lock	713266	The average lift of the 18th century locks	
Top Lock	712268	was 8½ ft, the average of all locks was	
* Leather Lock	702352	about 10 ft.	
* Hazle Lock	703359		

Notes:

A number of locks had alternative names.
* Destroyed by Gloucester-Ledbury Railway.
+ These were situated between Little Marcle Road and Bye Street, Ledbury.
Along with Over Lock, the last two were extremely deep, their 13 ft lift being almost a record for a narrow-lock in this country.
The summit level from Ledbury to Barr's Lock amounted to 10.2 miles.

Appendix Two

Industrial Archaeology

Surviving features of the canal excluding minor features and earthworks

Feature	Locality	Grid Ref	Feature	Locality	Grid Ref
Lock (remnants)	Over	817198	Bridge	Canon Frome	647423
Basin (restored)	Over	817198	Bridge	Canon Frome	644427
Culvert	Newent	727262	Bridge	Canon Frome	640430
Aqueduct	Newent	714265	Wharf House	Canon Frome	636431
Lock (restored)	Oxenhall	713266	Out-Building	Canon Frome	636431
Lock Cottage	Oxenhall	713266	Store houses	Canon Frome	635431
Culvert*	Oxenhall	706267	Crane base	Canon Frome	635431
Culvert*	Oxenhall	699265	Embankment	Canon Frome	632434
Bridge	Oxenhall	711274	Culvert	Stretton	630435
Stable?	Oxenhall	709277	Bridge	Monkhide	622438
Tunnel Mouth	Oxenhall	709277	Bridge	Monkhide	619438
Tunnel Mouth	Boyce Court	705297	Bridge	Monkhide	615438
Bridge	Boyce Court	703301	Bridge	Monkhide	613439
Embankment	Windcross	693325	Skew Bridge	Monkhide	612440
Wharf House	Ledbury	703368	Wharf House	Crews Pitch	608443
Wharf House?	Ledbury	708377	Store House	Crews Pitch	608442
Warehouse?	Ledbury	708377	Wharf House	Kymin	588450
Railway Bridge	Ledbury	706387	Lock (traces)	Kymin	581448
Bridge	Wellington	699401	Lock House	Withington	568441
Embankment	Prior's Court	696414	Bridge	Withington	567441
Aqueducts	Prior's Court	696414	Warehouses	Withington	555444
Sluice	Prior's Court	694415	Bridge	Sutton Marsh	546444
Half-Lock	Prior's Court	694415	Bridge	Sutton Marsh	543442
Wharf House	Staplow	692417	Bridge	Sutton Marsh	539441
Out-building	Staplow	692417	Bridge (remnants)	Sutton Marsh	537440
Bridge	Moorend	664415	Culverts	Sutton Marsh	536439
Bridge	Moorend	659416	Tunnel Mouth	Aylestone Hill	516416
Tunnel House	Ashperton	653418	Tunnel Mouth	Hereford	511415
Tunnel Mouth	Ashperton	653418	Bridge	Hereford	509413
Tunnel Mouth	Ashperton	650421	Bridge	Hereford	511408

Notes

1. Many of the sites are in private ownership.
2. Most of the buildings date from the 1830s or 1840s.
* Coal branch.

Acknowledgements and Sources

A history of this kind is not written without the help of many people, and I thank them all, a number of whom have sadly passed away since the first edition in 1979. In particular I am indebted to Stephen and Charles Ballard for making available various material including transcripts of their grandfather's diaries, also to Charles Hadfield for his Foreword and for drawing attention to the role of Maisemore Lock in the canal's final phase.

Members of the Canal Trust have also assisted, including Maggie Jones, Cliff and David Penny, Brian Fox, Brian Moult and Nigel Bailey. Thanks are also expressed to Gwladys Davies, B.J. Ashworth, Major R.E. Barnes, Theodore Baylis, the Hon. Edward Biddulph, Ray Bowen, Chris Clark, John Cornwell, Keith Falconer, George Hall, Michael Handford, Paul Hayward, Nigel Jefferies, Sinclair Johnston, John Van Laun, Dr M.J.T. Lewis, D. Mclean, John Norris, Harry Paar, Neil Parkhouse, Mike Potts, Peter Price, Fred Rowbotham, Andrew Shaw, Robert Simpson, Brian S. Smith, Robin Stiles, Rhodes Thomas, Dr Hugh Torrens, Jeremy Wilkinson and Ian Wright.

With regard to the sources, the Ballard diaries are of the first importance, thoroughly absorbing, and well deserve publication. Also, the company minute books will reveal more than I have had time to uncover. The Railway & Canal Historical Society's Cohen Collection contains an index of canal references in the Hereford newspapers, and other material consulted includes the following:

Gloucester Record Office	Maps, reports, Acts
Gloucester Library	Newspapers etc.
Hereford Public Library	Newspapers, Acts
Hereford Record Office	Ballard, canal material
Public Record Office, Kew	Company records

Some relevant publications are as follows:

Nigel Bailey, 2000, *Over and Over Again*
David Bick, 1987, *The Gloucester & Cheltenham Tramroad*
David Bick, 1987, *The Mines of Newent and Ross*
Anthea Brian, 1993, *Six walks Exploring the Lower Lugg Valley*
I. Cohen, 1955, 1959, Papers on local river navigations and the canal
Transactions of the Woolhope Naturalists Field Club
A. Farrant, 1977, *Rowing Holiday by Canal in 1873*
H&G Canal Trust, *The Wharfinger*
Charles Hadfield, 1967, *Canals of South Wales and the Border* (2nd edn.)
Charles Hadfield, 1985, *Canals of the West Midlands* (3rd edn.)
Heather Hurley, 1992, *The Old Roads of South Herefordshire*
E.T. MacDermot, 1927, *History of the GWR*
H.W. Paar, 1965, *The Great Western Railway in Dean*
Howard Williams, 1982, *The Diary of a Rowing Tour in 1875*

Index